CONFIDENCE

CONFIDENCE

BIBLICAL TRUTHS FOR DISCOVERING
GOD'S POTENTIAL FOR YOU

NORMAN
VINCENT
PEALE

Guideposts

New York

Confidence

ISBN-10: 0-8249-3220-X
ISBN-13: 978-0-8249-3220-6

Published by Guideposts
16 East 34th Street
New York, New York 10016
Guideposts.org

Distributed by Ideals Publications, a Guideposts company
2630 Elm Hill Pike, Suite 100
Nashville, Tennessee 37214

Guideposts and *Ideals* are registered trademarks of Guideposts.

Acknowledgments

Every attempt has been made to credit the sources of copyrighted material used in this book. If any such acknowledgment has been inadvertently omitted or miscredited, receipt of such information would be appreciated.

Scripture quotations marked (ESV) are taken from the *Holy Bible, English Standard Version*, copyright © 2001 by Crossway Bibles, a division of Good News Publishers. Used by permission. All rights reserved.

Scripture quotations marked (KJV) are taken from *The King James Version of the Bible.*

Scripture quotations marked (NCV) are taken from *The Holy Bible, New Century Version*. Copyright © 2005 by Thomas Nelson, Inc.

Scripture quotations marked (NIV) are taken from *The Holy Bible, New International Version*. Copyright © 1973, 1978, 1984, 2011 by Biblica, Inc. Used by permission of Zondervan. All rights reserved worldwide. www.zondervan.com

Library of Congress Cataloging-in-Publication Data
Peale, Norman Vincent, 1898-1993.
  Confidence : Biblical truths for discovering God's potential for you / Norman Vincent Peale.
     pages cm
  Includes bibliographical references and index.
  ISBN 978-0-8249-3220-6 (alk. paper)
1. Confidence–Religious aspects–Christianity. 2. Christian life. I. Title.
  BV4647.C63P43 2013
  248.4—dc23
                                                                    2013018253

Cover and interior design by Müllerhaus
Cover photograph by Shutterstock
Typeset by Aptara

Printed and bound in the United States of America
10 9 8 7 6 5 4 3 2 1

CONTENTS

FOREWORD

Thank you for your interest in the work of Norman Vincent Peale. We hope you'll find his words as deeply rewarding and potentially life-changing as we did. Each entry will be framed around one or more relevant Scripture verses, and discuss several conflicts, issues, occurrences, etc., that we face in the occasionally troubling world we live in. And each difficulty is responded to using carefully selected thoughts and anecdotes on the meaning and applicability of Scripture in daily life and the practical advice garnered from Dr. Peale's long life spent serving God and preaching His Word. The syntax has been slightly modified for our time but has preserved the true timelessness of Dr. Peale's original message of hope, toughness, and love, as well as his enduringly warm wit, knowledge, and affectionate presence.

—Editors of Guideposts

INTRODUCTION

Confidence. A word we all use often but many of us barely think about. I am not a slave to a dictionary, so I'll leave the semantics of definition to someone more learned than me, perhaps. I will say that the surest way to live confidently is to have what I call a "big God." Many of us, at different times in our lives, have a very little God. And make no mistake: it is we who have limited Him. We believe in God, but as to applying His power, His might, His love, and His greatness to our lives, we just aren't sold on the idea that it will work. So we have reduced God down to being practically a nonentity in our day-to-day lives.

If you have a little God, in the very nature of the case, you are going to get little spiritual results and little any kind of results. And with this little God, the problems common to all humanity can be counted on to gang up on you. But, on the contrary, if you think of a big God, if you pray to a big God, if you act like there is a big God, you will grow big spiritually and in every other way and big results will accrue. You will make a big contribution to the day and age in which you live. You will be a partner of a big God.

This may seem to you a rather extraordinary way to talk about God; but we are in good company, I assure you, for this is the way the Bible talks about Him: "The mighty God, The everlasting Father, The Prince of Peace" (Isaiah 9:6 KJV). Christianity speaks always in superlatives. St. Paul in his letter to the Philippians (4:19 KJV) writes, "My God shall supply all your need according to his riches in glory by Christ Jesus." Now what is meant by all my need? Surely, Lord, You mean by this that You will satisfy my spiritual needs . . . You are dealing with me only in spiritual things. But the statement doesn't say that. It has no parenthesis nor limitation. It says, "My God shall supply all your need." He will supply your mental needs; He will supply your emotional needs; He will supply your physical needs; He will supply your material needs. He will do everything for you—so it says in the Scripture. And by doing everything for you, you will receive, yes, confidence. The ability to believe in yourself, in something bigger than yourself, and it will allow you to do big things, with your big confidence, from your big God.

And again St. Paul affirms, "I can do all things through Christ which strengtheneth me" (Philippians 4:13 KJV). All things? You mean just some things, a few things. Oh no, it doesn't mean that at all. It means I can do—think of this! I, just a weak little human being!—can do all things through Christ who gives me the strength.

So don't sit around and wail and whine and moan and complain that you are weak, inadequate, and inferior, for that is not true at all, except only insofar as you insist on being that way. You say to yourself, "I believe in my God." Then you begin to grow into power.

What a God He really is! In the first days of every New Year it might be well to turn right back to the beginning of the Bible and start from there. How does the Bible begin? Well, everybody knows. "In the beginning God created the heaven and the earth" (Genesis 1:1 KJV). No little God did that, because this is a tremendous earth and this is a tremendous solar system. And He made it all. He took His great hands and scooped out the deep valleys and raised up enormous mountains. Then He took both hands and grabbed handfuls of stars and swung them into the blue. All space is filled with them. And He started rivers singing their way to the sea. He designed the universe so that there would be sunset and sunrise and high noon, and spring and summer and fall and winter, and He brought into being the productivity of the earth.

Men from this planet have now gone to the moon. And what did they find when they got to the moon? They found that the same laws that are operative on earth are operative on the moon. They could do the same things there that they can do here. And for the first time in the history of mankind human eyes beheld not the rising of the moon or the rising of the sun, but the rising of the earth. Those men were so enthralled that they repeated these words from Scripture:

> In the beginning God created the heaven and the earth. And the earth was without form and void; and darkness was upon the face of the deep. And the Spirit of God moved

upon the face of the waters. And God said, Let there be light: and there was light. And God saw the light, that it was good: and God divided the light from the darkness. And God called the light Day, and the darkness he called Night. And the evening and the morning were the first day.

And God said, Let there be a firmament in the midst of the waters, and let it divide the waters from the waters. And God made the firmament, and divided the waters which were under the firmament from the waters which were above the firmament: and it was so.

And God called the firmament Heaven. And the evening and the morning were the second day. And God said, Let the waters under the heaven be gathered together unto one place, and let the dry land appear: and it was so.

And God called the dry land Earth; and the gathering together of the waters called he Seas: and God saw that it was good.

—Genesis 1:1–10 KJV

Mankind affirms the greatness of God. And we affirm the greatness of God with our confidence. We have a big God and if we live up to a big God, which means generosity and brotherhood and kindness and goodwill, this big God will make big and confident people and a big and confident society of people who know their God. They shall be strong, strengthened through Jesus Christ who sustains us. Amen.

—Norman Vincent Peale

PRAY BIG, THINK BIG, BELIEVE BIG

Then he touched their eyes, saying, "According
to your faith be it done to you."

–Matthew 9:29 ESV

There is a three-point formula that can change your life. This formula has power in it, plenty of power. We should never forget that the possibilities inherent in a human being are limitless. Anything you can dream of and aspire to, that is in harmony with the will of God, you can obtain.

The particular formula to which I refer was given to me years ago by an old man who, to my way of thinking, was one of the wisest, most acute human beings I ever knew. He was a successful businessman, but he gave away most of the money he made and thus he blessed the lives of thousands of people. He had profound insight and understanding and I learned a great deal from him. When I first knew him he was about eighty and I was in my twenties.

At the beginning of my ministry I was shy, inordinately shy, even to the point of shrinking. I had a big inferiority complex and was trying to preach an enormous, tremendous Gospel, but I was neither enormous nor tremendous in my faith.

One day I went to see this old man at his farm, tucked away in the Tully Valley, amidst the hills of upstate New York. He gave me a lecture that I still recall, although, God help me, I haven't followed too well. In the course of that lecture he asked, "How big is the Gospel you have undertaken to preach? Are you preaching a big Gospel?" And then he gave me the three-point formula: "Pray big, think big, believe big." And he continued, "If you faithfully practice this, you will be given insight, wisdom, courage, and strength."

Just what is meant by praying big? Well, my old friend said the trouble with many people is that they pray little, inconsequential, indifferent prayers. They will never get a big answer from God unless they pray big to God.

I recall one night years ago I made a speech in Cedar Rapids, Iowa, and had the great honor of being on the same program with one of the most illustrious singers of our time, Roland Hayes, a deeply spiritual man of great erudition and faith. I was charmed by his singing and by him personally. The next morning he and I rode into Chicago on the same railroad train, through a blinding snowstorm. I shall never forget the inspiration of the conversation I had with him. Among other things, he told me about his grandfather, who lived in the South way back in slavery days or shortly thereafter. Roland Hayes himself was a cultured, intellectual man. His grandfather, on the other hand, had practically no book learning but was well-schooled in the Scriptures. I shall always remember the way Roland Hayes described his grandfather's prayers, using the old man's language, "The trouble with most prayers is: they ain't got no suction."

What a picturesque phrase, meaning, I presume, that many prayers don't go down deep enough, they don't come to grips with the problem, they have no pull to them, they are weak and ineffectual. "They ain't got no suction." This, when you take and apply it to your own problem, means that if you can't move the problem, maybe the trouble is that you haven't prayed big enough or with enough vigor and strength.

Of course, this is quite contrary to the kind of religious teaching now in vogue. A good many church leaders, heaven help us, are trying to reduce Christianity to a nice little thing from which they have almost completely erased the supernatural element. The old greatness of faith that our fathers used to know and practice is gone. And in its stead there remains a weak, little, allegedly rational kind of faith, so insipid that it isn't even rational.

But over against this trend, consider the magazine *Guideposts*, which perhaps you read. There are only a few magazines with larger circulation. Theoretically, *Guideposts* shouldn't succeed. It is not sold on newsstands, only by subscription. But it succeeds anyway. And the reason is that it has faith. It is an interfaith magazine and a magazine of faith. It believes in deep, big prayers, for one thing. There was a story in *Guideposts* about a missionary's wife. The scene: the city of Shenkiu in central China—Henan Province. It was at the time of the Japanese invasion of China during World War II.

The Japanese were approaching this city; they were very near—only two or three days away. The Chinese colonel came to the mission compound and told the pastor's wife that she had better leave, as he had received orders not to defend the city against the Japanese. The pastor, a medical missionary, had been taken to a hospital, himself ill. He was a hundred and fifteen miles away and would not be back for perhaps a month. His wife was by herself, with a baby girl two months old and a son just over one year.

There began an exodus from the city. The elders of the church came and invited her to go with them to their villages. They were very kind and gracious people. But she had these two babies, and she knew that the village homes of these people were vermin-infested and full of germs. Western babies lacked the necessary immunity. There had been many deaths among missionaries' children exposed to conditions in the villages. Therefore, this missionary's wife was afraid to take her babies into those houses. So she remained in the city, alone, one American woman with two babies. The gatekeeper, her last protection, came and said that he too must leave. The poor woman was filled with fear, alone, unprotected, in bitter January weather, with the enemy approaching.

She went to the kitchen sink to fix a bottle for the baby. Her hands were cold. She shook so from fear that the bottle almost fell from her hands. Then she saw above the sink the Bible-text calendar. It was January 16, 1941, and beneath the date she read these words from Psalm 56:3: "What time I am afraid, I will trust in thee." She was astonished, but strangely comforted. All that night she kept her two little ones huddled close to her to keep them warm. She lay awake, listening to the wind rattle the paper windowpanes in the bamboo frames, praying to God who, all the time she was afraid, would be with her. It was noon before she remembered to pull the page off the little daily calendar. The tenth verse of the ninth Psalm read: "And they that know thy name will put their trust in thee: for thou, Lord, hast not forsaken them that seek thee." As she bowed her head over her noonday meal, she thanked God for those particular words at that moment.

When the following morning came, she realized that she was without food. All the stores were empty or closed, for there was no food coming in from the countryside. All she had were the goats, but she did not know how to milk them. Once again, fear clutched at her throat. How would she feed these children ? She pulled off the calendar page for January 17 and, believe it or not, under the date of January 18 were these words: "I will nourish you, and your little ones." Genesis 50:21. This modernly trained woman, schooled in the new thinking, asked herself, "Is this only a coincidence?"

There was a rap at the door. It was a little Chinese woman, Mrs. Lee, a longtime neighbor. "We knew you would be hungry," she said, "and you didn't know how to milk the goats. So I have milked your goats. Here is milk for your children."

Presently another little woman came, holding a live chicken by the legs and also carrying some eggs. Once again the pastor's wife looked at the words, "I will nourish you, and your little ones." That night her heart was full of hope. To the sound of shells bursting in the sky, she prayed that somehow God would spare the city and the gentle people whom these missionaries loved.

The next morning she rushed to the little square of paper hanging on the nail and tore off the page. "When I cry unto thee, then shall mine enemies turn back: this I know; for God is for me." Psalm 56:9.

This time it seemed too much to believe! Surely a verse chosen by chance for an English calendar couldn't be taken literally. And another fear clutched her. The Japanese army—what would they do with one lone, defenseless woman? She went through her husband's papers, destroying any that might be construed to incriminate her. She could hear the sound of gunfire coming closer and closer. She went to sleep that night fully dressed, prepared at any moment to meet the Japanese invaders.

She awoke in the early dawn expecting to hear rough shoes on the gravel, marching troops. But instead there was a deep quietness. She cautiously went to the gate and watched as the streets began to fill, not with Japanese soldiers, but with townspeople coming back into the city. The colonel reappeared and said to her, "We don't understand it. The Japanese were headed for this city. They were going to take it. Suddenly they turned aside. We didn't defeat them. They just went another way and left us unoccupied."

Will you try to explain this away, handle it on an intellectual basis? I could do that too. I could rip it all to pieces as just pure coincidence. But when you come right down to it, what is coincidence? It is an act of God in the midst of time.

Right this minute the supernatural power of the infinite surrounds our thinking. This generation has actually had the audacity to dispense with the infinite. They have tried to make God just a nice little God who cannot act outside our rules. What a pretty little God they have tried to make of the great God of all eternity. Some people have erased Him so far in their minds that they say He is dead. What this country, what this world, needs is a new emphasis on the power and might of the eternal and everlasting supernatural God, Who can be reached through big prayer. When your little prayers do not reach Him, get some suction into your prayers. Dig down till you find Him or climb till you reach Him.

The second part of the formula is to think big. Now this is very important. I have a quotation from Lord Chesterfield that we might well ponder: "Think great thoughts. You will never go any higher than you think."

How high do you want to go? If you can only think to the rooftop, that is as far as you go. But you can think your way illimitably to the stars. And what you think will be. If you think little, you will get a little result, in the very nature of the case. If you think big, you will get a big result. What you are now is what you have been thinking for a long time. What you will be ten years from now depends on what you think from now on. If you want a great life in the future, think great thoughts.

A preacher friend of mine came to see me and started pacing the floor, saying, "I want to describe the church I hope to have someday." He pictured very graphically a church surrounded by fifteen acres of land, made of glistening steel and glass, that would seat a congregation of three thousand people. He described a soaring ten-story tower, in which there would be carillon bells. He pictured it all meticulously, specifically, to the smallest detail. He got me so excited that I leaped to my feet, exclaiming, "The church is already built!"

"What do you mean, 'The church is already built'?" he asked.

"It is built in your mind," I said. "All you need do now is to finish the job."

Ten years later I dedicated his church. As I drove around it, looked at it from a distance, heard the carillon bells ringing out, I saw that this was in precise detail exactly what he had described to me out of his mind ten years before. Now if he had projected in his mind a little church seating one hundred and fifty persons, that is what he would have had. But he is one of those rugged souls who believe in God and the Lord Jesus Christ, one who prays big and who thinks big. What do you want to build out of your life? Project it in your mind.

Pray big. Think big. I would stop at this point, but I referred to a three-point formula and even made it the title of this sermon. So I must give you the third point. The first point is pray big. The second is think big. And the third: believe big.

This is Christianity any way you take it: "According to your faith be it unto you." That is from the Gospel of Matthew, chapter 9, verse 29. In other words, your life is going to be in proportion to how greatly you believe. Believe little, you get a little life. Believe soft, you get a soft life. Believe weak, you get a weak life. Believe fear, you get a fear life. Believe sickness, you get a sick life. Believe big, and you get a big life. Jesus said, "All things are possible to him that believeth" (Mark 9:23 KJV). Which means what? That the person who believes is going to get everything he wants? No, it doesn't say that. But it does mean that if you believe big, you move things out of the realm of the impossible into the realm of the possible. Christianity is the religion of the incredible, the religion of the astonishing, the religion of the breathless. You bring to yourself what you believe.

Some people believe that life isn't much good, that they aren't much good, that they can't do much with their lives, that they are defeated—and they accept the defeat. They believe that that is the way it is always going to be. They hear about a boundless God, but they have only little, narrowly circumscribed lives, which is an astonishing tragedy. You have to gear yourself to believe big. A couple consulted a minister friend of mine in California. His church is located near the shore and this couple had been coming each Sunday to hear him. He preaches a big, boundless, generous Gospel. "God wants to pour out blessings on everybody," he says, "but a lot of people fail to get these blessings because they block themselves off from them. Consequently, they live on a little trickle of blessings, when they ought to have a river of blessings."

Having listened to this preaching, these people, husband and wife, went to the minister one day and said, "We don't understand why it is that we are poverty-stricken. We have money trouble all the time. You talk about the boundless generosity of God, but we never see anything of it. We're just living from hand to mouth." And they asked, "Will you pray for us?"

"Well," the minister said, "I'll pray for you if you'll do something for me." And he gave them the strangest thing to do. "I want you to take tomorrow off. You've done so poorly with your jobs that one day off won't hurt. I want you to go down to the beach and spend several hours there counting grains of sand. Get yourselves a big handful of sand and count every grain. Then see if you can calculate how many grains of sand the Lord has made. When you get tired of doing that, look out at the ocean and see if you can figure how many fish God has put in the ocean. Then try to figure how many gallons of water there are in the Pacific. When you get tired of considering the sand and the fish and the water, take a walk through the park and count all the leaves on the trees."

This strange device was to show these two people the prodigality of God. "I just want you to realize," the minister told them, "that this God Who has put all the sand on the beach and all the fish in the sea and water in the ocean and leaves on the trees is trying to put blessings into your life. But you're closed. Your belief is too little."

Well, they got the idea. They went and talked it over with God. And they began to reappraise their lives. They forgot their expectations of impoverishment. They began to see new possibilities; new ideas came to them. They started an enterprise that brought new values and new prosperity into their lives. They learned to believe big, pray big, think big, and accordingly built themselves a full, rich, satisfying life.

I have preached bigness today. Why not? Christianity comes from a big God, a big Savior, to make big-minded, big-souled people. Remember the incredible fact: "All things are possible to him that believeth." That is true—a big, marvelous truth. Pray big, think big, believe big, live big.

HOW TO BE AN ASSET TO YOURSELF

And a certain man was there, which had an infirmity thirty and eight years. When Jesus saw him lie, and knew that he had been now a long time in that case, he saith unto him, Wilt thou be made whole? The impotent man answered him, Sir, I have no man, when the water is troubled, to put me into the pool: but while I am coming, another steppeth down before me. Jesus saith unto him, Rise, take up thy bed, and walk.

–John 5:5-8 KJV

Are you an asset or a liability to yourself? Are you helping yourself to live a creative, good life? Or are you constantly hampering yourself, getting in your own way?

This is a very serious question, because people often are, to use the old phrase, their own worst enemies. If you stopped to count how many times in your life you have frustrated yourself, it would give food for thought. How many times have you defeated yourself, tripped yourself up? If anybody else did to you what you do to yourself, you would consider him your worst, most implacable, most vicious enemy. Our problem isn't anybody else, primarily. Our problem is ourselves. James M. Barrie said, "What really plays the dickens with us is something in ourselves." And Shakespeare wrote, "The fault, dear Brutus, is not in our stars, But in ourselves, that we are underlings."

Have you ever asked yourself, "Just what in the world is wrong with me anyway?" Well, if you haven't, I can tell you that I have.

I have been pastor at the Marble Collegiate Church for a long time, and I have some long memories. Strange thing about the human mind, you will forget certain things for a long time and then they come back to you. Recently I thought of an encounter that, I tell you, I hadn't thought of for many years. Perhaps what brought it back was this theme of being an asset or a liability to oneself—I do not know. But one day years ago I was sitting in my study when my secretary came in and told me there was a couple outside who wanted to be married. We have couples who just wander in like that, with a marriage license, and want the ceremony performed. I asked, "Is the license in proper form, all the questions duly answered?"

"Yes," she said.

"Well, let the sexton go ahead and prepare for the ceremony. I'll be glad to take care of this, but I would like to see the couple first."

"I think before you see them you might examine the license," she advised.

I looked at the license and saw that the woman's name was that of one of the most famous motion picture actresses of that day, known to everybody. But the license showed that this would be her fourth marriage—the other three having been ended not by death, but by divorce.

"You know, I can't do this," I said to my secretary.

"Why don't you see them," she suggested.

They came in. I do not believe this woman is still living—I have not heard her name in years. Such is fame that your name can be splashed across theaters all over the world and then be seen no more. And you are gone, by death, old age, retirement, or whatever. At any rate, it has been a long time since I have heard this woman's name. But when she walked into my study that day she was one of the most beautiful women I ever saw in all my life. Striking, magnificent, with a commanding presence and at the same time a beguiling sleekness. She had very keen eyes. She had brains, this woman did.

And I said, "It is a pleasure to meet you. Your acting has given me much pleasure. I think you are one of the greatest. God has given you an enormous talent, which you have used with great skill." She graciously acknowledged this. Then I said, "I can't do this for you, though." I looked at the character she had with her. While I never like to disparage anyone, and may have underestimated this man, he did not appear to me to be in the same league with her. I thought, *Why this man?* But then you never know, do you, why people marry whom they do. I often wonder why my wife married me, for that matter! She probably wonders herself.

"I am not surprised at your decision," the actress said. "I came to you because . . ." And she was kind enough to say I had written a few things that had helped her. "I just thought perhaps you might," she said, "but knowing your position as a minister of the Gospel and knowing the Bible as I do, I can understand. I respect your honesty in telling me that you cannot perform this ceremony."

So we all shook hands and I wished them well. Then she sort of gave the high sign to her proposed husband to go on out ahead of her, which he did with alacrity. This may have been one reason she selected him. At any rate, he departed. Shutting the door, she looked at me and said, "Look, I was brought up as a good Christian girl. I love the Lord. Will you please tell me what is wrong with me?"

"Well," I answered, "I wouldn't undertake such a thing with the time we have at our disposal. I do not know what is wrong with you."

"I have been told that I am too beautiful." Then she added an interesting thought: "There are great liabilities to being beautiful."

"Maybe there could be a glorious asset in it if to physical beauty there were added a deeper beauty."

"Ah, yes," she said, "that has always been my conflict. There is something wrong in me. I don't know what it is."

"Why don't you come and talk sometime?"

"Oh, it would be no use," she continued. "I am caught in this. I'm in a different world than you are. What is it in me?" With that she left me and closed the door. And maybe not only the door. I never saw her again. Maybe somewhere she did find peace. Could it be that as her fame passed she found humble peace? I don't know. But here was a woman who was saying, in effect, "How can I be an asset to myself?" Each of us has something inside that plays the dickens with him. How is it healed, how is it exorcised, how is it brought under control? How does one cease to be a liability and become an asset to oneself?

One of the most marvelous passages in all the literature of the world is the beginning of the fifth chapter of the Gospel of John, the first eight verses. More is said about psychology and psychiatry and therapy in those eight verses than in many five-hundred-page books. The skill of the writers of the Bible to penetrate to the essence succinctly is one of the wonders of the ages. That is why the Bible lasts while other books molder away. The story that is told in these eight verses is about a man at the Pool of Bethesda. And what was the Pool of Bethesda? Well, it was a pool in Jerusalem at the time of Jesus. I myself have actually put my hand in the waters of the Pool of Bethesda, but today you have to go down thirty feet to reach the water. The Jerusalem of Jesus' time is anywhere from twenty to sixty feet below the surface of the present city. The first great destruction of Jerusalem came in AD 70, when the Emperor Titus leveled it to the ground, changed the name of the city, and obliterated every religious site, thinking he could blot it out forever. Even the city that was reared on that one was later destroyed. Over the centuries, rubble upon rubble, foot after foot, the surface rose—until now the level where Jesus walked is anywhere from twenty to sixty feet down, depending upon the declivity of the terrain.

Well, here was the Pool of Bethesda. It was by the sheep market, and poor, miserable people came there to lie around in the porches. There were no hospitals in those days. There was no Great Society to take care of these people. There was no one to alleviate their misery. There were no orphanages, no homes for the incurable. There was nothing. They just lay around the pool in these porches.

But there was hope because of the tradition that at times an angel would come along and disturb the water. If you were lucky enough to be the first to jump into the water after the angel had disturbed it, you would be immediately healed. We know today that there are naturalistic causes. And the water is still troubled, whether by an angel or by naturalistic causes I wouldn't know.

There was a man near this pool who had been hanging around for thirty-eight years, waiting for a chance to get into the water after it was troubled. You would think, wouldn't you, that sometime in thirty-eight years he could have contrived to be the first one in? He could have got right at the edge and lain there and let people feed him, and the minute the water was troubled he could have rolled over and flopped in. But you see, the trouble was that he didn't really want to be cured. He wanted to stay in that same misery that he had always been in, like an old lady who told me one time she'd been "enjoyin' poor health." It is a fact that people after a while get to like the miserable way they are. Human nature is complex.

Well, Jesus walked along and saw this fellow. He knew very well that the reason why the man did not want to get into that pool and get healed was that he had been there thirty-eight years, longer than anyone else, which made him chief man at the pool. He had status; all the newer ones would say, "Look at that old boy. He's been here thirty-eight years." He had built himself up; he was the big shot at the Pool of Bethesda. But he was miserable. Jesus, with the most astute mind ever to come into this world, knew this man inside and out, just as He knows you and me inside and out. You can't fool Him. You can fool other people; you can even fool yourself, but not Him. So He came to this man and asked, "How long have you been lying around here, old boy?"

"Why," said the man, "I've been here thirty-eight years. There is no one who has been here longer than I."

Maybe he expected Jesus to say, "Now, isn't that great! We ought to put you on television. You've been here all this length of time—you ought to be written up in a book or something because you have been here such a long time."

Instead, Jesus said, "Look at Me." The man had his eyes down. Jesus said, "Look at Me!" Slowly the eyes came up and they looked into those eyes. (I often wonder what the eyes of Jesus looked like.) Anyway, those eyes caught the eyes of this man. Jesus looked him through and through and said, "I want to ask you a question. Do you want to be made whole, really?" The man looked at Him and was about to make more excuses. But Jesus repeated, "I'm asking you straight. Do you want to be made whole?"

Something was pulled up out of the soul of the man by the look of the Great Healer and in that minute he reached for it—he grabbed and said, "Yes." In that minute he was made whole. Jesus said, "Pick up that bed you've been lying on all this time. You won't need it anymore. And get going."

This is the most modern story you can read today. There are people this very day lying impotently on their beds by some Pool of Bethesda, yet not needing to be the way they are. The question is, do you really, with all your heart, want to be an asset to yourself? That is the question. If you do, it can happen to you.

The first thing I would suggest doing is something that will not be any fun. You're going to be glad when this sermon is over! It started out being embarrassing because of my first question; now it is going to get really tough. The thing to do is sit down and ask yourself, *What is my greatest weakness, my greatest fault?* Do you know what it is? Or has your mind, which always has a tendency to rationalize, blocked it out so you do not know what your chief weakness is? I wonder. I imagine when you really start evaluating, you know what it is. If you know what it is, and if you want this liability eliminated, it can be eliminated. Years ago I taught on the subject "You Can Be Strongest in Your Weakest Place." That idea is based on an analogy from welding. If you take two pieces of a broken metal object and weld them together under intense heat and then take a big sledge and try to break that object, it may break, but very likely it will not break at the point where it is welded, because due to the powerful heat applied at that particular point, the metal has become strongest at its weakest place. That also happens when an individual comes under the profound heat of Jesus: he becomes strongest where he was the weakest.

On the Sunday when I preached on this subject, there was present a man who had a terrific temper. He was a contractor. He had such a bad temper that he would always avoid getting into business negotiations personally, for fear he would get angry and say things that would upset the deal. He would send an assistant to negotiate for him. When he played golf, he would take along a half-dozen extra golf clubs, because if he made a poor shot he would wrap the club around a tree. His was an ungovernable temper.

So this man sat in church that day and heard me preach. After church he and his wife walked up the street—he told me about it later—and when they had gone a little way, he asked, "Mary, what is my greatest weakness?"

Well, Mary was a smart girl and she had been around a long time with this character. She answered, "Why, sweetie, you have no weaknesses at all."

"Well, I'll tell you something. You've got one. You're the biggest liar I ever met. You know my temper, don't you?"

"Yes," she admitted, "I know your temper. What a man you would be if you were under control!"

"Well," he said, "that minister said I could become strongest in my weakest place. And that is exactly what I am going to do."

He came to see me. I sent him to my dear old friend Dr. Smiley Blanton, the psychiatrist, one of the wisest, kindliest, most understanding human beings I ever knew, who has since gone on to heaven. And with Smiley's help, the man began to understand the deep source of his temper: inferiority feelings, repressed hatred of a father who had mistreated him as a little boy, and related inner tensions. Self-knowledge is the beginning of wisdom. Smiley then referred the man to a little book by Dr. Loring Swain, which stressed the point that to control temper, for example, you have to want to be through with the luxury of getting angry.

Presently Dr. Blanton pointed out to the man that he could continue working psychiatrically with his tangle of inferiority and resentments, but it would be a long process and that there was one Doctor Who could heal him and do it quickly. That doctor was named Jesus Christ. The contractor committed himself to Jesus, and I am not exaggerating one iota when I tell you that he never lost his temper again. He was still a spirited man, but he was under control for the rest of his life. The change came in one instant of time, as soon as he really wanted to change. You are never going to change unless you really want to. Do you want to be made whole? That is the question. If you do, then determine what your biggest liability is. You don't need to tell your minister or your wife or husband. Just tell yourself. And tell the Lord. Tell Him what you would like to be and He can make you that. It is a big assertion, but I would not make it unless I truly believed. You name the kind of person you would like to be, name what you want to do in the world, and Jesus can lift you to it. He takes what little we are, or what great we are, and steps it up.

I have had a wonderful time recently reading the book *Movin' on Up*, by Mahalia Jackson, the great gospel singer. She tells in her book that she was born between the railroad tracks and the levee in New Orleans. When the railroad trains came by, she says, the house shook, like it was going to fall down.

The people along the levee used to sing old songs, mostly hymns, many of which had been derived from popular songs in London during the development of the Salvation Army. Mahalia Jackson loved to sing them. She sang at the laundry work she did to help support her family—getting no schooling after the eighth grade. On Sundays she would sing at the Baptist church.

At sixteen Mahalia went to Chicago in hopes of earning a better living. She was a maid in a big hotel for a while. She sang as she made beds.

Twenty-five years later, a great banquet was given in the same hotel, one of the most beautiful in the country, at which Mahalia Jackson sang gospel songs to the musically elite of Chicago. She sang in the Sportpalast in Berlin; she sang in the Vienna Opera House; she sang in Royal Albert Hall in London—to vast multitudes of people everywhere, singing the songs of the Lord.

A group of musical experts in New England wanted to analyze her singing. They asked her about her technique. She said, "I have no technique except that I love the Lord."

She herself says that what lifted her out of her lowly beginnings in New Orleans was—what? the voice? "No," she says, "it was the Man I am singing about. If He could lift me from the washtubs, He can lift you up too. But you cannot do it yourself. You have to let Him lift you up."

So, are you going to spend your life being a liability to yourself? Or will you let Him lift you up?

BETTER WAYS TO BETTER DAYS

Whoever would love life and see good days must
keep his tongue from evil and his lips from
deceitful speech. He must turn from evil and
do good; he must seek peace and pursue it.

–1 Peter 3:10-11 NIV

It would appear that a good many people today are dissatisfied with life and profoundly dissatisfied with themselves. Now
there are many proper reasons for being dissatisfied with con-
temporary civilization, but that isn't what I have in mind at this
moment. Of course, unless there were constantly in each suc-
ceeding generation a creative discontent, things would become
static and without progress. But the dissatisfaction of many
people today is underscored by something that has pathologi-
cal overtones to it. There is widespread exasperation, ranging all
the way from common irritation and annoyance to dramatic life
failures. Untold thousands of people are reaching for better ways
to better days. As an example of the dramatic aspect of all this,

and I might add the pathetic aspect as well, I have a typewritten note found by a congregant of mine on the sidewalk. Here is the way it reads:

"King Heroin is my shepherd, I shall always want, He maketh me to lie down in the gutters. He leadeth me beside the troubled waters. He destroyeth my soul." Now whoever wrote that had, I would say, a fair amount of graphic and tragic genius. And on the reverse side is handwritten the following postscript: "Truly this is my psalm. I am a young woman, twenty years of age, and for the past year and one half I have been wandering down the nightmare of the junkie. I want to quit taking dope and I try but I can't. Jail didn't cure me. Nor did hospitalization help me for long. The doctor told my family it would have been better, and indeed kinder, if the person who first got me hooked on dope had taken a gun and blown my brains out. And I wish to God she had. My God how I do wish it."

This is representative of thousands of people today who, never having heard the clear, authentic word on how to live life and find it good, have taken the road that leads only to a dead end. This, of course, is a superdramatic example. But how many people are there right around us who long for better days, days of more peace, more goodness, more happiness, more love, more brotherhood; and who constantly seek and wistfully wish for better ways to better days? How can better days be brought about? Do you want an answer about how to live? There is one place to find it—in the pages of the Holy Bible. This is a book that is alive; there is vitality, there is excitement, there is exultation, there is greatness, there is life on every page. And the Bible writers knew how to "tell it like it is." Long before this modern phrase was invented, the Bible writers were telling it like it is. So how do you find good days? It is very simple. In 1 Peter, the third chapter, you will find this statement: "Whoever would love life and see good days must keep his tongue from evil and his lips from deceitful speech. He must turn from evil and do good; he must seek peace and pursue it."

There it is, take it or leave it, says the Bible. It is either-or. If you want to be happy, if you want to have good days, just skip the evil and go for the good. The evil is wrong, and when you do wrong everything goes wrong; but the good is right, and when you do right things turn out right. It is just that open and shut. Then the Bible, which is a straightforward, honest, man-sized book, goes on to indicate you'd better do what it says, but warns that there is nothing soft about it, nothing evasive. It simply tells what is going to happen if you go for the evil: "The eyes of the Lord are on the righteous and his ears are attentive to their cry; the face of the Lord is against those who do evil" (Psalm 34:15 NIV).

That sounds old-fashioned, doesn't it? Well, that is the way it is. Remember, the Bible does not guarantee freedom from pain, sorrow, trouble, difficulty, and heartache, but it does promise inner happiness and good days. So to have better ways to better days, keep all this in the background of your mind. Here are one or two suggestions for accomplishing it. First, live honestly. How many people do live with absolute honesty? Have you ever been completely honest with yourself? Have you ever told yourself the whole truth about yourself? Have you ever faced yourself, not as you think you are, but as you really are? How long has it been since you made an appraisal of your strengths and your weaknesses? Do you know whether you are deteriorating or whether you are growing? Are you a better, more confident, more knowledgeable person now than you were ten years ago—or are you a worse person now than you were ten years ago? Honesty is the first principle for having better ways to better days.

A very good thing to do is to sit down with yourself and ask, *What is my worst weakness?* Don't ask your wife what your chief weakness is. She'll probably name a half dozen. Don't ask your husband. He could come up with a few. Just ask yourself, *What is my chief fault?* When you find it, then study it. There it is. Maybe you have had it for years. Maybe it is the thing that has been holding you back from better days. But, once having isolated it, once having faced it honestly, you can decide what you are going to do about it, with the help of the Lord Jesus Christ. A person who is really honest with himself and has isolated his faults and taken them to God can do something about them. And, when a real fault is out of your way, what glorious better days you can have! The greatest person in the world is an absolutely honest person (although sometimes he is not the most pleasant person in the world!). And when you can help another human to get honest with himself, he is on the way to having something happen to him.

For example, I had a little exchange of letters with a doctor who lives near Nashville, Tennessee. He is an old friend of mine now. But this is the way our friendship began. He wrote me a letter. I happened to write a newspaper column that appeared in about two hundred newspapers throughout the country and apparently he had been reading my column.

He wrote: *Dear Dr. Peale: I have read every article by you that has appeared in my local paper and I wonder how many people are more unhappy in their lives, more mixed-up, after reading them. The trouble is, you say that whenever anything goes wrong all you need to do is to pray about it and have faith and everything will turn out right. Now I don't agree with you. I think in this life you either get the breaks or you don't get them, and that a lot of people who don't get them could have done just as much good if not better with the same breaks as the people who got them. I don't think or believe that any Supreme Being has a thing in the world to do with any of it. You and your talks lead a man to think that prayer and faith can do absolutely anything, and I want to tell you that that is a lot of bunk and you know it. Sincerely yours.*

Now that is what you might call a man-sized letter, and when I read it I didn't like it too much. But then I got to thinking, Here is an honest man. This letter was written on the 18th of August and I didn't answer it until August 25. It's sometimes a good idea not to answer a letter like that right off the bat; just wait a little while.

So, after praying about it, I wrote him: *Dear Doctor: It was very nice of you to write to me. Even though you take exception to my articles and in fact are aggressively opposed to them, nevertheless I was glad to hear from you. I have never been the type of person who likes a "yes man." In fact, I would almost rather get the kind of letter you wrote than a complimentary one. I would just like you to know, Doctor, that I absolutely believe what I write. It is not written out of theory, but on a basis of facts which I have observed and personally experienced. You are a scientific man, and I will guarantee that if you will put these principles into practice with an open mind, an objective attitude, they will work for you also. With kind regards, I am, Cordially yours.*

And we developed a nice correspondence. Then one night I went to Nashville and made a speech in a civic auditorium there. Afterward, back home, I received this letter:

Dear Dr. Peale: I had to drop you a short letter and this is written between patients. I was in Nashville last night and had the pleasure of hearing your lecture. I wanted to meet you but got there too late, as I brought some Alcoholics Anonymous down and we just left too late for me to try to see you. This thing called power and faith I have put to work and, believe me, it works. Some of the results you get are absolutely uncanny. I can't believe some of the things that have happened; still, they did happen. I just wanted to drop you this note to tell you that prayer and faith absolutely work. Yours sincerely.

Well, maybe I had better success with this man than with some others. But the point I want to make is that, even though he had a hostile attitude, it was evident that he was honest. He wasn't satisfied with what he was. He knew his faults. He wanted to be a different individual. He was reaching for something better, and he fought back because he was being challenged. We recognized this honesty and liked him for it—in fact, loved him for it. As we brought him to Jesus Christ he started forsaking evil and doing good, with the result that he found better ways to better days.

So, suggestion number one is: Be absolutely honest. The next thing is to be absolutely un-stereotyped. Now what in the world do we mean by that? Just this: Each human being is born as an individual, absolutely free within the great area of God's love. But as we grow from infancy to childhood and young manhood or womanhood we get rolled together into a mass. We are taught to talk alike, to think alike, to act alike, with little or no variation from the standard, and the result is that the lilting, growth-seeking personality is stultified and frustrated. We tend to become what we read in the newspapers or what we see on television. We pick up the jargon of the day. We dress according to the styles some character in Paris happens to think up in order to sell more clothes. One time we had long skirts scraping the ground. Then we had miniskirts scraping the elbow. But they have to keep varying the styles in order to sell more goods; so next comes the emphasis on the maxi-skirt. The same is true in men's clothes; wide ties, narrow trousers, colored shirts, we all follow along docilely.

What a pity that human beings who were meant by Almighty God to be free should become victims of this tendency! Actually it doesn't matter a whole lot what you have around your neck or on your body, or whether your hair is long or short, so long as it's an expression of your individuality and not subservient cliché that crushes the personality that God meant you to have, to be free. So if you want better days, a better way to get them is to be firmly and freely yourself, as a child of God. God is a great individualist. He is not a dullard. He could have stamped out a lot of faces like Coca-Cola bottle tops, but He gave each of us an individuality different from anybody else's. So be your own great wonderful self. You are an immortal soul.

This is what we all, deep down, are reaching for: to burst out from behind our masks and be the released people that God put it in our hearts to be. You are a free spirit. You must not let anything hold you down—your weaknesses or disappointments or prejudices. You must take wings and live free—and be on your way to better days.

EVERY PROBLEM CONTAINS ITS OWN SOLUTION

Open my eyes that I may see wonderful
things in your law.

−Psalm 119:18 NIV

The crowds on the streets of an English cathedral town were going about their ordinary daily activities. Suddenly someone spotted a woman standing on a narrow ledge high on one of the towers of the cathedral. A great crowd gathered below, hushed and horrified. Policemen at once climbed the tower and attempted to bring her down. A minister came and talked with her, asking that she tell him whatever was on her mind. But after some thirty minutes of indecision, she flung herself from the tower down onto the street. Nobody found out what problems had driven the woman to her desperate act. But there is one thing she apparently didn't know, or to which she gave no concern. It is the great, powerful truth that for every problem there is an answer. Or, to put it another way, every problem contains the elements of its own solution.

One of the wisest statements ever made on this subject—one I have quoted before, I am quite sure—was made by a member of Marble Collegiate Church. It is a classic. This statement was made by Stanley Arnold, one of the top idea men of this country. He services a number of the great industries of the United States with sales and merchandising ideas and his services come very high, because he is a thinker. He thinks up ideas and he knows how to phrase them. This one is worth its weight in gold if you could weigh it. "Every problem," he says, "contains the seeds of its own solution." Not the seeds of its dissolution, but the seeds of its solution. As I say, I've quoted that before, but perhaps it ought to be repeated from time to time until at last the truth of it really grabs us—the truth that right at the heart of any problem, however difficult it may seem, is buried the solution thereof. Now, when you are talking about thinking and ideas and truth, church is the right place to be, because the Bible is at the center and it is quite a book.

Every smartness that has ever existed is in its pages. It is full of ideas that are as modern as tomorrow morning's newspaper. In the 119th Psalm, the eighteenth verse (KJV), is this one: "Open thou mine eyes, that I may behold wondrous things out of thy law." What law? Why, the basic law of the universe. Not the law of aerodynamics or the law of mechanics, but the law of God, the law of the mind, the law of the soul, the law of the spirit. "Open thou mine eyes, that I may behold wondrous things out of thy law." One of these wondrous things, and it is truly a wondrous thing, is that every problem that you or I can have contains the seeds of its own solution. So you don't need to feel defeated or overwhelmed by any problem you may have, because the solution is there if you will open your eyes to find it and see it. The ancient thinker Epictetus wrote, "When you have shut your doors and darkened your room, remember never to say that you are alone, for you are not alone; but God is within and your genius is within." What a truth! So what is your problem? Hold it out there in front of you and give it a good looking over. Rip it apart; break it up. Dissect it; analyze it. And right at the center of it, buried like a gem, is its solution. "Well," you say, "that's great, but how do you do it?"

Let us suggest three principles for so doing. First, *think!* Really think. Second, *believe!* Really believe. Third, *pray!* Really pray. There you have three dynamic principles and with those principles you can, I do believe—in fact I know—find an answer, the answer, the right answer to any human problem. Let us take that first one. Think! Let me ask you something. How long has it been since you really thought? I might ask that of myself. When did I last think? I don't like to think. Do you? It's painful. It is one of the most painful exertions known to man, thinking, deep thinking. And we shrink from it. We like to be relieved of the necessity of it. So we think off the top of our heads. And the trouble with those thoughts off the top of the head is that they do not go down into the depths. But when one gets over the first hump of really thinking, gets into the area where it is creative, actually it's a delightful and exciting experience. John Burroughs, one of the greatest naturalists this country ever produced, probably the greatest, said he felt that there are just two classes of people in the world. He said that he didn't mean men and women, or young and old, or rich and poor. They weren't the classes to which he referred. The two classes in his mind were what he called the quick and the dead. By the quick he meant people who look at the world and see it, people who listen to the world and hear it, people who get a message from it. The quick are people who are sensitized; they send out antennae. They get the meaning of the world. In other words, they are alive, they are alert, they are vibrant. Those are the quick. As for the other people, while they aren't dead physically, they are dead from the standpoint of sensitivity. They never grapple with ideas. They never try a new way of doing something. They are dead in the spirit. They live on the surface. So there are two classes, the quick and the dead.

Now the quick are the people who can think. I maintain, and I know it can be demonstrated, that you can think your way, with the help of God, out of any crisis, out of any situation, out of any problem, if you get your eyes open and see the wondrous things that are in His law. Oh, there are so many illustrations of this! But let me give you one. Recently my wife presented me with a set of the sermons that I have preached in the Marble Collegiate Church in the past twenty years. She had them bound in a series of nice volumes—volume one, volume two, and so on, beginning in 1950. That's a lot of sermons. And she put them in my office. I don't know whether she put them there for enlightenment or for decorative purposes. The color of the bindings does fit in with the décor, you might say. Well, I was very impressed by these volumes and I thought I'd look and see if I could find anything inside that was impressive also. Now bear in mind I was reading my own sermons—which shows to what extremity I was reduced. But I picked up the volume for 1951 and read one of the sermons there and, you know, even though I say so myself, it wasn't half bad. At least I found in it the story of an incident that I had long since forgotten, but which is really a beauty of an example of how to think in the face of a tough problem.

When I talk this way, I know some of the people sitting out in front of me are thinking, *Look, you don't know how tough my problem is*. Well, that shows that you are thinking, but you are thinking negatively. This was the story: It seems that there was a couple by the name of Husted who lived in a little town in South Dakota called Wall—population, I guess, some five or six hundred. This was back at the time when there was a great drought all over that part of the country. There were days on end without any rain and the soil was finely pulverized. The winds would catch it and sweep it up in great dust clouds, forming what was known as the great Dust Bowl. This caused one of the greatest migrations in American history—a migration of people who could no longer get any value out of a farm. Farm prices fell to nothing. People were ruined. There was poverty everywhere, all over that whole region. Now this Mr. and Mrs. Husted ran a drugstore in their little town and under such conditions, as you can well imagine, the drugstore business wasn't going very well. So one day when the temperature was 100° in the shade, they were sitting there with no customers coming into their store. They were facing financial ruin, although they never admitted that they were, for they knew that there must be some way out.

They sat at the front window with their chins in their hands, watching people rolling along on the highway, which wasn't well paved, so there were great clouds of dust. There was no car air-conditioning at that time, so you had to keep the windows open. And the dust was sweeping into these cars. Mrs. Husted said, "Here is the proposition: We have something for these people in this store. How can we make them know that we have something for them, so that the two of us will get together?" You see, all the cars just passed rapidly through that little one-horse town. Now I have developed this at great length in order that you may see a problem in which you might think there wasn't a ray of hope. But this woman was a great Christian. She had great faith. She had her eyes open to see wondrous things in God's law. So she prayed, she believed, and she thought. And she asked herself, *What would those people out there at this moment, with one hundred degrees in the shade and this dust, like to have more than anything else?* And the answer came to her out of her head as she was thinking: *What they would love to have is a big glass of ice water.*

So she and her husband made signs. They went 100 miles on either side of the town and put up signs along the highway, then at fifty miles, and twenty-five miles, and ten miles. They made big signs that said, "To all passing motorists: There is a free glass of pure, delicious ice water awaiting you at the Wall Drugstore. Wall, South Dakota. Hold on until you can get to Wall." Later they even went as far east as Albany, New York, and put up a sign saying, "For a free glass of ice water—the Wall Drugstore, Wall, South Dakota, 1,725 miles farther on." Did people flock to the drugstore? Of course they did. It wasn't long before Mr. and Mrs. Husted had twenty-five clerks, not only handing out ice water but selling merchandise as well.

This is the point: what do you mean, you can't find an answer to your problem? The trouble is that oftentimes we won't acknowledge that there is a possibility of a solution. We even get a little irritated if anybody tells us that our problem is not without solution. There is a solution to any problem. It doesn't necessarily come easy. Of course not. But if you practice those three principles—think, really think! believe, really believe! and pray, really pray!—the result will be that your eyes are opened and you see wondrous things in God's law. And His law is what? It is the law of prosperity; it is the law of abundance; it is the law of goodness; it is the law of love. And it is just full of creative possibilities and potentials, just full. The Lord wants to give you everything. You won't be able to get it, however, unless you think, unless you believe, unless you pray. But if you do, then you will find the solution to any problem. With the second principle—believe, really believe—the question is: how deeply do we believe? Do we just believe off the surface of the mind? In the book of Jeremiah (29:13 KJV), we read, "And ye shall seek me, and find me, when ye shall search for me with all your heart."

Nobody ever made anything great out of his life who didn't do it with all his heart. I remember talking years ago with a motion picture star whose name would be known to everybody. I knew that she had had a great deal of trouble in her life. I asked, "How come you keep at it with such enthusiasm?"

"Why," she answered, "because I love it. I give my whole self to it." And she did. She wasn't any raving beauty, but she threw everything she had into it. If with all your heart you give yourself to your business, to your children, to your marriage, to your future, to your hopes, you are going to come out with something that is lasting and strong. Believe. That's it. Not long ago I addressed a luncheon of the National Association of Manufacturers in the Waldorf-Astoria Grand Ballroom. There was a huge crowd, including most of the great businessmen of this country. And I got into a conversation with someone who said, "There is a man here you would like."

I remarked, "I seem to like all the people I'm meeting here."

"This man is a special case," he said. "Talk about trouble, poverty, difficulty! He had it. But, in spite of all, he won through and has created a great enterprise." So naturally I sought the man out. I had only two minutes with him and asked this question, "What is the secret of your success?"

He began to disclaim but I persisted, "No, give me the facts. I know you've done a great job. How did you do it?"

"Well," he replied, "there were times when it looked as though the business might fold, but I never let go of my belief in it. I just believed it into greatness." And that's another phrase that might be called a classic. "I believed it into greatness." So, whatever your job, believe it into greatness. If you have a child or a young person who may be giving you a little bother, just believe him into greatness. Believe everything into greatness.

"Open thou mine eyes . . ." Oh, what a passage that is! "Open thou mine eyes, that I may behold wondrous things out of thy law." Law is the way it works scientifically. Think, really think. Believe, really believe. There is no limit to the power of believing. The third principle, pray, really pray, is like the first two. It is effective, not by surface application, but only as you pray in depth. The mumbling of ritual prayers without probing their depth of meaning and applying them to everyday problems will not solve your difficulties. It is only as belief turns into prayer that the answers come and God's power is brought into a situation.

Let me tell you about a little incident that happened a good many years ago in the Midwest, in a farmhouse of the kind from which most of America originally came. A boy seventeen years old was desperately ill. He had pneumonia. In those days pneumonia was a sinister disease. It is nothing to trifle with even today, but now we have drugs that can fight it successfully. There were no such drugs in those days. You survived, if you did survive, because you had basic good health or because you asked God to give you life. Medicine in those days could help, but it was not decisive. Well, it was late at night and this boy was lying there in a coma. The doctor said, "This boy is really healthy and strong and his lungs respond to a certain degree. I see no reason why he should die. I'm baffled."

He sat there in his shirtsleeves, studying the boy. The clock on the wall was ticking, the parents were huddled together, the younger children were frightened, and the neighbors were concerned. Finally the doctor said, "What this boy needs is a transfusion." They all immediately responded, "We'll give blood."

"No," said the doctor, "it isn't a blood transfusion that he needs, but a faith transfusion, a desire to live. In some way he is near death because the faith isn't there to pull him through."

What a doctor! He said, "If something doesn't happen in the way of a transfusion like that, he will die before morning." Well, there was an old farmer there who had his Bible in his hand, a great big hand grown strong from struggling with the earth, cradling the Bible lovingly. This farmer was a believer. He had no university education in the usual sense, but he had gone to the university of the Bible. He was a simple man and he took the Bible as it was. He took the promises of God as they were. He just accepted them; he didn't doubt them; he believed in them. He had the faith of a little child. When the doctor said the boy needed a faith transfusion, he drew near to the patient. He put his mouth down close to the boy's ear and started reading him great passages out of the

Bible, with the thought that he was driving them into the boy's unconscious mind, trying to reach the center of control. The hours passed and he read on. The clock continued to tick. The doctor paced the floor. On and on, hour after hour, the farmer drove those healing thoughts into the boy's unconscious mind until finally, when the first faint streaks of dawn came, suddenly the boy gave a sigh, his eyes opened, he looked at the man and at all the people in the room—gave them a big smile and fell into a deep, untroubled, normal sleep.

The doctor felt his pulse, checked the vital signs, and with tears in his eyes said, "The transfusion has succeeded. The crisis has passed. The boy will live!" And he did live. Saved by what? By faith and prayer and thought. The problem had its solution right within itself as all problems do. "Open thou mine eyes, that I may behold wondrous things out of thy law." Think, really think! Believe, really believe! Pray, really pray! Then, no matter what the problem, you will be capable of finding the solution contained inside of it, like a diamond in the rough.

HOW TO STAND UP TO A TOUGH SITUATION

Commit thy way unto the Lord; trust also
in him; and he shall bring it to pass.

–Psalm 37:5 KJV

How to stand up to a tough situation . . . There you have a subject
that everyone, including the speaker, needs to know about. And an
answer to this may be given in one sentence, or it can be enlarged
into a whole discourse. The one sentence is very simple, but if it is
believed in and used it can help you stand up successfully to any
tough situation, no matter what kind it may be. This may seem
like claiming a great deal, but the claim is a valid one. The sentence
is found in the fifth verse of the thirty-seventh Psalm, one of the
greatest truths ever enunciated. Here it is: "Commit thy way unto
the Lord; trust also in him; and he shall bring it to pass." Reduced
to modern language, that means: Don't struggle so hard. Don't get

yourself worked up. Don't fill your life with tension. Do the best you can with any situation and then commit it—that means put it completely in the hands of the Lord, trusting absolutely in Him, and He will bring it to pass in a right and proper manner. This is an old truth, but the wisest and most astute of men and women have believed it, have applied it, and have found it will absolutely, positively work. It is a strange thing how tough situations seem to get us all down. But they don't need to if we get a right and creative attitude toward them. Maybe right now you are thinking, *Brother, you don't now what a tough situation I'm facing.* Well, that is great. We have a great answer for you. And this great answer will match your great need.

A friend of mine, a minister by the name of Charles Boonstra, was out fishing with his son. I don't know how old the son was, but, judging from Charles's age, I would estimate between nineteen and twenty, or maybe seventeen or eighteen. The two of them must have been in pretty good communication with each other, because as the father described rather negatively and at great length a tough situation that he was facing, the boy listened for a while and then gave his father an answer, which in my humble judgment is a classic. This one statement alone is worth all the trouble you are taking to hear or read this sermon. He said to his father, "Oh, knock it off, Dad. Remember this day is the first day of the rest of your life!"

Now how in the world he ever thought of that, who knows? But the father said it penetrated his dark mass of unhappiness and cleared the air. *If,* he said to himself, *this is the first day of the rest of my life, I'm going to get going and I'm going to do it good! I have the power, with God's help, to handle this tough situation.*

Which he proceeded to do. An important part of handling a tough situation is to personalize it as something you have to deal with, almost invest it with a personality, and stand up to it. Don't let yourself be overwhelmed by it. Put it out there by itself. Look it in the eye and bring up your resources. Do as a man I heard about who was faced with a very tough situation and felt it was getting him down. In the middle of the night he did some praying and he did some Bible reading and he did some thinking—and those three things taken together will wrap up an answer to anything. It came over him that through the power of the Lord he could handle this thing. He went out on the lawn of his house and he visualized his tough situation standing there in front of him and he personalized it and spoke to it, saying, "You stand there. I want to talk to you." He put his hands on his hips and he spread his feet wide apart and he said to that tough situation, "You have no power to hurt me at all. Do you get that? And I have what it takes to handle you! I'm going to commit my way unto the Lord; I'm going to trust in Him; and He will bring it to pass."

What you've got to do once in a while, you know, is to stand up and remember who you are. You're a man. You're a woman. You're not a weakling. You're not a worm. You're a child of God. Don't be pushed around by a situation. Start pushing situations around with strength and with power. "Well," you say, "that sounds all right, but it's rather oratorical and bombastic. How do you actually do it?"

Here are a few suggestions. One: Don't fall into the error of being influenced by people who gloomily tell you that you must face the facts. Obviously the facts are important, but don't be overawed by them, because facts can and do change. So don't have your eyes only on the facts. Get your eye fixed on something that doesn't change: the wisdom and the power and the love of God. Take your eyes off the facts and put your eyes on God. Let's just explore this business about how "you've got to face the facts." I've heard that said so many times. Here is a man about fifty-five years of age who loses his job and doesn't know where to get another one. A well-meaning friend comes around and says, "Jack, let's face it. When you're fifty-five it's pretty tough to get another job. You might as well face the facts."

Now, if enough people say that to Jack, he is likely to settle for facing the facts. Or here's a couple who fell in love, got married, raised some children, and then began to grow apart. They tell their friends all about the conflicts they are having, and some well-meaning person says, "Well, you might as well break it up. You'll never get together again. You might as well face the facts." And so you could go right down the line with a negative treatment of every situation. But in each of these a wise friend would say, "Yes, sure, this is tough and you may have some difficulty and there may have to be some give-and-take and some struggle. But be thankful we have a big God, and He will help you to straighten out that situation and overcome the facts."

The important question is: How much are you willing to trust God? I tell you, friends, I honestly believe that if you trust Him completely, with all your heart, you'll never go wrong. And why should you trust God? Because He is right. He is rightness itself. He is the truth. There is no error in Him. And if you stay with Him there will be no error in you.

So, when trouble comes to you, don't just face the facts—face God. Another thing is to think big, believe big. The bigger you believe, the bigger the results will be. Do you want a little result? I can tell you how to get a little result: Think little, believe little, and you'll get a little result. Think big, believe big, and you'll get a big result. Even God Himself can't give you or me any more than we are mentally and spiritually conditioned to receive. He gives to us in direct proportion to what our thoughts are, what our faith is. You know, the Bible isn't only a holy book; it is the world's greatest gathering of scientific principles on how to live. Sometimes these principles are set forth in strange ways and you have to dig to find them, but they are there.

For example, in the second book of Kings there is this story about a man named Elisha: Elisha had a disciple who died and left his widow in impoverished circumstances. After a while the widow got so that she had practically nothing. She came to Elisha and said, "I am really up against it. I have nothing in the house and I have many debts. My creditors even now are threatening to come and take my children as satisfaction for my debts. I'm desperate."

Elisha asked, "What have you? Have you anything at all?"

"I have a jar of oil," she answered. Now oil was and always has been a precious commodity. Elisha said, "All right. I'll tell you what you do. Go to all the neighbor women and borrow vessels. Borrow as many empty vessels as you'd like to have filled with oil, and take them to your house. Later I'll tell you what to do."

So she went out and borrowed some vessels, but not very many. Her faith was small; she was thinking small. Then Elisha said, "All right now. Take your cruse of oil and start pouring it into these vessels."

She did and the oil kept on flowing until all the vessels were full. Only when the last vessel was full did it stop flowing. Maybe there are people who would write this off as some kind of magic. They don't understand that in this is buried a principle. And what is the principle? Simply this: Our thoughts are vessels, our ideas are vessels, our prayers are vessels, our faith is a vessel—and, depending upon how big we make the vessels, God pours His illimitable resources into us. If you come up with only some timid, little thought, then you get a little poured in and you complain, "I can't live on that!"

And of course you can't. But if you develop your thoughts until they are huge, if you believe that God's generosity is absolutely unbounded, if you live with Him in your big thoughts, then He will support you with His marvelous blessings. That is the principle. It has worked for hundreds of years; it is workable now. And I know people who work it.

One morning last summer I was in Teheran, in the lobby of the hotel. It was Monday morning. I mention this because it is important to my narrative. The night before I had preached to a wonderful congregation of English-speaking people living in the city of Teheran. Now it was Monday morning and I saw walking through the lobby an amiable-looking, friendly gentleman who smiled as he approached me. His swarthy complexion made me think he was an Iranian, but I didn't know. We had had no words up to this point. Presently he asked, "Are you an American?" "Yes, sir," I replied. He told me he'd been living in Illinois for quite some time. He had left Iran sixty years before to set up business in the United States, and now he was on a visit to the old country. He asked, "Did you hear Dr. Peale at that church last night?" Right away I could see he didn't know me. "Yes, I heard him," I admitted. "How did he do?" he said. "Well, to tell you the truth, he didn't do too well," I said. "That's strange," he replied. "I heard him once and he did pretty good. I guess he must be slipping."

Well, I finally enlightened him and we became good friends. I said, "What business are you in, sir?" "I am in the oriental rug business. I've been buying rugs in Teheran for years and selling them in the Midwest." He handed me his card, which said, "Oriental Rug King."

"My friend," I said, "I have a problem, and maybe you can help me. My wife says that she is not going to leave Teheran without buying a small Isfahan rug. I've tried to talk her out of it, but I haven't succeeded, and I don't know where to go to get a rug."

"Oh," he replied, "don't you go. You wouldn't know how to do it. You go with me." Now, friends, never in all my life have I seen such bargaining genius as this man displayed. It was worth the price of two rugs to watch him work. On the way back to the hotel we talked some more and he told me that his being in Iran this time was not just to buy rugs.

"I'm here," he said, "to build a church in my native village. I'm going to pay for it all myself. I'm going to build a church to the glory of God. I was a poor boy with no opportunities, but, fortunately, in my early years I was taught to believe—and the more I believed, the more God poured blessings on me. So I'm going to help pour out His blessings on more people."

So get out the vessels, all you can find, every thought you can muster, and open them all and let God pour His oil down in them. Commit unto the Lord; trust also in Him; and He shall bring it to pass. That is the message.

Now the third thing I want to recommend to you is to employ the power of prayer. This is hard to get across, because everybody agrees with me. But do you agree enough to join in a recognition of the kind of prayer we are talking about? It is not just mumbling a little prayer off the top of your head. Even that is good, but it doesn't carry much power. The kind of prayer that gets big results, big enough to handle tough situations, is continuous, agonizing prayer in depth. That kind of prayer releases forces and powers that are indescribable. I have seen people pray themselves out of and pray themselves above the most terrible difficulties, the most difficult problems, the greatest hardships. But this has been through deep, sustained prayer that drives down into the consciousness.

Long ago my wife and I were entertained by President and Madame Chiang Kai-shek in Taiwan. We went up to their summer home at Lishan, which is a distance from Taipei, the capital, traveling on that marvelous cross-island highway, one of the greatest road-building achievements I have ever seen anywhere in the world. And there we spent the late afternoon and evening and stayed until the next morning with these friends whom we have known for many years.

I have never seen any change in this man. Time seems to have no effect on him. There isn't a wrinkle in his suntanned face. His eyes are lustrous and soft and clear and he wears no glasses. He stands lithe and straight. He has an infectious smile and laugh. He is sharp and keen in his conversation. He seems to have a kind of eternal youth. I asked him, "Mr. President, at eighty-plus, how do you stay so healthy, so vibrant, so alert? What's your secret?"

"It's a simple secret," he answered, "but it is also a costly secret. Just pray three times every day."

Madame Chiang, who was sitting nearby, said, "But, Norman, it's the kind of praying you do. It's not for two minutes and not for ten minutes. My husband prays, meditates, thinks, and surrenders to Christ for thirty minutes three times every day. That is an hour and a half of praying every day. And he has given orders to his associates that, no matter what the circumstances are, he is never to be disturbed when he is at prayer and meditation."

The next morning I awoke at 5:30. From my bed I could look out the window and see a red-lacquered balcony. (The place is built in the old Chinese style.) There I saw Chiang Kai-shek walking up and down. He was wearing a long black cape and a cap, for it was cold, and he was followed by two huge dogs. He had his hands together and his lips were moving, so I knew he was praying. It was his first half-hour prayer period, at 5:30 in the morning. And later, before we departed, we stood in a circle holding hands with the president and his wife as again prayer was offered. There is power in this world, great power, that can be ours if we are willing to pay the disciplinary price of prayer in depth. "Commit thy way unto the Lord; trust also in him; and he shall bring it to pass." Then you can say to any situation, "You have no power over me at all. I can handle you." Even the toughest situation. With God's help, it isn't so tough after all. Amen to that.

WHY THE CROWDS LOVE HIM

I, when I am lifted up from the earth,
will draw all men to myself.

−John 12:32 NIV

It's a pastoral cliché to say that I want to talk about the most exciting person who ever lived, about the most lovable man who ever
walked the earth, about the greatest brain that ever strayed into
human history, about the most incredible personality who ever
came among us—of course, I'm talking about Jesus Christ our
Lord. No one can leave a spell over our hearts as can Jesus. No one
can enthrall us like the Nazarene. There's truth in every cliché, as
the saying goes.

I attended a church service some years ago in Lucerne,
Switzerland. It was an Anglican Church, the only English-
speaking Protestant service in that Swiss city. The congregation,
therefore, consisted not only of Anglicans and Episcopalians, but
of members from all American denominations. The preacher was

CONFIDENCE

an Englishman with a real English accent. He gave the ritual-
istic part of the service beautifully, using the ancient, sonorous
prayers, which he recited impeccably. Then he crossed from the
reading desk to the pulpit and suddenly he became a different
personality.

This man was an old army chaplain. He changed at once from
flawless English into the vernacular. I can see him yet, a great raw-
boned fellow, as he leaned over the pulpit and shook his finger at
the congregation and said, "Now look, friends, I am going to talk
to you about the best friend you ever had. I'm going to talk to you
about the One who understands you better than anybody on this
earth. I'm going to talk to you about the One who can bring the
best self out of you. You better listen to me. And you better love
Him. I'm going to talk to you about Jesus Christ."

Sitting there where through the window I could see Mount
Pilatus shouldering out the sky, I was aware of a hush that settled
over the congregation as this man talked in direct, simple English
about the One Who is more loved than any personality who ever
entered into human life. Strange, the effect He has on people! I've
seen strong, tough men grow misty-eyed when you talk about
Him. I've seen congregations melted down by Him.

This happens also in other situations. In a certain American
city the Lions Club sponsored a Lenten Season presentation. I
came across it when, walking through the city park, I saw a long
truck from which came religious music. On the side of the truck
was a sign stating that inside *The Last Supper* was depicted in wax.
And it went on to say that this was presented by the Lions Club,
admission free, but voluntary offerings would be used for some
charitable purpose.

The idea of seeing *The Last Supper* in wax did not particularly appeal to me. I've been to Madame Tussaud's wax works in Times Square, and you never quite get the feel of a personality in wax. But at any rate, since it was free, I thought I'd go in.

There were with me the following, standing quietly and beholding *The Last Supper*: an indescribably dirty little boy, of about six maybe. His hands hadn't had any affinity with soap and water in a long time. Even his face was dirty. But he was lovable. Then there was a couple. They both had long hair and at first it was difficult to determine which was the boy and which was the girl. They were of the hippie type. The boy had on a leather jacket with a kerchief around his neck. The girl had on a mini-mini-skirt. Last, there was a feeble old man, and myself. We all stood there looking at *The Last Supper*.

The figure of Judas was exquisitely done. You could see the greed, clearly depicted in the wax. And there was Simon Peter, strong yet weak, both elements showing on his countenance. But it was the figure of Jesus in the center that caught our attention. He was portrayed as I like to see Him, not as a delicate man, but as a very strong man. And there was on His countenance a look of deep love and compassion. The background of music was: "On a hill far away stood an old rugged cross. . . ."

Suddenly I began looking at my companions. The little boy was gazing up with his mouth wide open, a look of wonder on his face. The old man, although bent, was looking intently and long thoughts were revealed in his expression. The young hippie couple, holding hands, were lost in contemplation. All of us were caught and held by Jesus.

As we left we made our offerings. I was just after the little boy. He grubbed down into his pocket and came up with a nickel, which he placed in the box. My one-dollar contribution seemed insignificant in comparison and therefore I increased it to two dollars and even that didn't seem enough. As we walked into the street, into the bustling crowds of a modern American city, we were all under the spell of a Man who had lived over 1,900 years ago in the flesh, but who lives today no less. Let us think back to that first Palm Sunday long ago when Jesus came into the capital city. He did not come on some great white horse preceded by troops and guarded by an FBI. He came in on a donkey. Now the donkeys of the Holy Land are very small. They are not much bigger than large dogs. One time when in the Holy Land I had a great desire to bring one of them home with me. Even though I am not too tall, my feet would almost surely scrape the ground riding on one. Jesus must have had to tuck His feet up when He rode on that donkey. For a lesser man it might have looked ludicrous, but when He rode it was the King of Kings coming, the Son of David, the Savior of Mankind. He had an inexpressible power and dignity in His personality. There has never been anyone like Him.

When He spoke, people asked, "Where did this man get these words?" No man ever spoke as He did. And the crowds shouted acclaim for Him. You can go through those crowds in imagination and see some of the biblical characters who must have been there, individuals for whom He had done immense things. Naturally they loved Him and they shouted for Him. And there have been people shouting for Him all across the years. We shout for Him today too.

But we must stop just shouting for Him and do something for Him. I think one of the greatest tragedies in the history of the Christian Church is for followers of Jesus to be inactive in these present days. There are thousands of churches in this land that have taken what they call His principles and proceeded to propound them, but have forgotten Jesus Himself. His principles are the greatest ever to be enunciated. They come from the greatest mind in all of human history. They are the blueprint of the future. But you never reach the masses of people with principles alone. The secret of the victory of the Christian Church across the ages is and has been Jesus Himself.

The Bible tells us that He said: "And I, if I be lifted up from the earth, will draw all men unto me" (John 12:32 KJV). Hold Him up and people can't resist Him; they can't turn away from Him. He not only has a great intellect; He not only knows the score; He not only has the truth; but He puts out His arms in love to all mankind, no matter what they do. The Bible relates that one time when He spoke the multitudes sought to touch Him. Think of that! The whole multitude, listening, reached forward to touch Him—not touch His idea, but touch Him, ". . . for power came forth from him and healed them all." Why wouldn't the crowds shout for Him?

For another thing, Jesus gives us the power to overcome any tragedy, any difficulty, any problem in this life. I don't know what your problem may be today. Willa Cather, the great author, said, "There are only two or three human stories. . . ." Basically, there are only a few human problems, and they are all represented here today, I am sure. Turn to Him and He will give you the power to overcome. There is unlimited power in Christianity if you really go for it. Most people are content to take it superficially and get merely a superficial effect. During the same visit to Lucerne, I was writing a book, and I was sitting on a terrace, a place where the mountain slope dropped off sheer for about five hundred feet.

I liked working there because the view was magnificent from that point. The man who owned the hotel where I was staying came along and asked me what I was doing, and I told him that I was writing a book about faith. "I'd like to tell you about my father. You know, this whole hotel complex was built by him." His father was Fritz Frey, one of the greatest hotel men Europe ever produced. His son went on, "When my father was a young man fortunately he had an accident and had to spend a year in the hospital."

"Why do you say, 'fortunately,' Mr. Frey?"

"Because," he replied, "up to that time my father was a careless believer, but during that year he read the Bible through several times from the beginning to the end. And as he read he became acquainted with Jesus. Jesus became the great obsession of his life. My father had such faith that he could walk on the very edge of this precipice and not be afraid. He was never afraid of anything, from then until the day he died, because he lived with Jesus."

One of the greatest Americans who ever lived died recently. Some commentator at the time of his passing compared him, as a military man and political statesman, to George Washington. But of all that has been written about Dwight Eisenhower, I like the statement made by Lyndon Johnson the best. He said, "A giant of our age is gone." Eisenhower was also one of the most lovable men I have ever known. He was great, but he was humble—which is partly why he was really great. One day I well remember I was offering prayer at a big meeting in North Carolina and President Eisenhower was on the platform. I had to go way out ten or twelve feet to the edge of the rostrum to give the prayer. I felt somebody come up beside me and I opened my eyes for a moment. It was the president. He didn't want to stand in back. He came up and prayed right along with the preacher. It was touching; it was real. He was a man of God.

Once I had the esteemed privilege of a little visit with him, in the course of which I asked him who was the greatest person he had ever known. It was perhaps a curious question, but I thought it was a good one. Besides, I wanted to know. He replied, "The greatest person I ever knew? Oh, that's easy, very easy. It was my mother.

"Now," he continued, "my mother was a devout Christian. She believed in Jesus. All my family did. My mother never had more than a few years of formal schooling, but she was very wise. She went to school to a great Book, the Holy Bible, which gave her perception, understanding, insight, and wisdom.

"And oftentimes," said he, "since I've been in this job as president I have wished that I could go to my mother. When I've been lost in problems, or over what to do about certain men, I have thought, *If only I could go to my mother!* She understood men; she understood problems. But she has been gone these many years and I miss her.

"One cold winter night," he continued, "my mother and we boys were playing cards together in our Kansas farmhouse. Now don't get me wrong. My mother was very straight-laced. She didn't play with the kind of cards that have kings and jacks and queens on them. She wouldn't have them in the house. This was an old-fashioned card game called Flinch, but, like all card games, it started with the dealing of a hand.

"Well, my mother dealt me the worst possible hand and I began to complain. Finally she said, 'Boys, put your cards down. Now you, Dwight, especially, since you're complaining so much,

I want to tell you something. Look, that hand was dealt to you in love. It's just a game and your mother dealt the hand. But when you get out into the world you're going to be dealt many a bad hand with no love in it.

"'Now,' she said, 'I don't want you to complain. Remember that you are an American and you are a Christian—and that, no matter how hard your adversity, God and the Lord Jesus will help you. So you just play out the bad hands you get, confident that the Lord will see you through.' And He has," he concluded. Dwight Eisenhower was a lover of this great figure who gives you the power to handle all the difficulties and tragedies of life.

Another reason why millions love Him is that He loves us. Do you think anybody loves you as He does? Your husband loves you. Your wife loves you. Your children love you. Your mother loves you. Your father loves you. But nobody loves you like Jesus. He is your everlasting friend. He will see you through this life and receive you to glory. He is a faithful friend. He will never fail you. He will never let you down. The greatest thing Jesus offers is love.

If our society would finally get smart and turn to Him, we would solve our problems. But we still are so stupid, despite our sophistication, that we believe the world can be changed by force. Anybody and everybody who ever tried to change the world by force failed. Even if you win a war, you don't "win the peace." You've got the same problems on your hands. You really move humanity by just one thing, love. And Jesus is the one great figure of all time who has that most. He teaches love. He is love itself. So we love Him because He loves us. Let me conclude with this: I had a letter recently from Luther B. Bridgers Jr., of Atlanta, Georgia, who asked me if I remembered his father, Luther Bridgers. And indeed I do, for meeting him and hearing him tell of the tragedy that struck him early in his life was an unforgettable experience.

I was in Georgia to give a talk and was entertained for dinner at the home of Luther Bridgers. He was a Methodist preacher down in South Georgia. As a young man he had a beautiful voice. They say he was a singer who could move you to tears. And he married a beautiful girl and they had three children. Now, he was an evangelist and went around to various towns to lead revival meetings. He was a great preacher. And one day when he was leaving home on his way to conduct a two-week meeting somewhere, he looked back before he went around the corner and there was his sweet wife, with a baby in her arms and by her side two little boys. And they waved, "Good-bye, Daddy." And he went off.

Well, on the last night of that two-week meeting, at one o'clock in the morning, he was called to the telephone and a friend at the other end of the wire said, "We are sorry to tell you, but your house caught fire tonight and burned, and your wife and children have been burned to death."

Bridgers dropped to his knees beside the telephone, crying to God, "Lord, I have preached this Gospel to other people, and have told them it would comfort them in every hour of sorrow. Grant that this same Gospel may comfort me."

Almost instantly, he said, he felt great strong arms around him. He told me, "The feel of those arms was as real as your presence here this evening." He carried the agony of that terrible bereavement for months and years, but the love of Christ gave him victory. He continued preaching. Eventually he remarried.

As he finished telling this story there in his parsonage in a Georgia town, he went to the piano, saying, "Let me sing you a song I wrote sometime after." And he sang an old gospel hymn that I've heard many times and maybe you have too. I hadn't known it was he who wrote it, but there was his name at the top of the piece. Now quite near the piano there happened to be a canary in a cage—a beautiful yellow canary. And as Luther sang this bird sang. I'm not attuned much to the intricacies of music, but it seemed to me that the bird and the man were absolutely in harmony. The bird was singing at the top of its voice, and so was the man. And the look on the man's face—well, it was wonderful to behold. And this is what the man sang:

There's within my heart a melody
Jesus whispers sweet and low,
Fear not, I am with thee, peace be still.
In all of life's ebb and flow.
Jesus, Jesus, Jesus—
Sweetest name I know,
Fills my heart with longing,
Keeps me singing as I go.

It is for this reason that human beings in the hard pathways of life have loved Him and shout acclaim for Him, for they know that at long last it is He Who will give them peace and victory. So let's really stand by Him. It is an honor to be a part of that crowd.

KEEP BELIEVING— NEVER LOSE FAITH

I had fainted, unless I had believed to see the goodness of the Lord in the land of the living.

—Psalm 27:13 KJV

Some time ago I was talking with a gentleman who seemed to be on top of the world, as the saying goes. He was filled with vibrancy. He gave the impression of being 100 percent alive—which can't be said of everybody, that's for sure.

His attitude astonished me somewhat, because through the years I knew how much trouble he had been through. You've heard it said, "It never rains, but it pours." Well, it really poured upon this man. But despite everything, he endured it all and, more than that, he surmounted all of it victoriously. There was happiness, vitality, even excitement in him. "You are a remarkable, undefeatable, indefatigable human being," I told him. "You really are something special. How come?"

He grinned and said, "The answer is: Years ago I bought the message preached in Marble Collegiate Church, and with it evolved a philosophy that will stand up under anything. Nothing can break it—and I mean nothing. And it can be stated in five words: Keep believing—never lose faith."

That man is only one of the hundreds, even thousands, of people for whom Marble Collegiate Church, with its message of the Gospel of Jesus Christ, has made all the difference between victory and defeat, joy and despondency, hope and despair.

While reading in the twenty-seventh Psalm I came across these words: "I had fainted, unless I had believed to see the goodness of the Lord in the land of the living." What a picture that sentence gives of a man who was really up against it and would have fainted and folded had he not been able to see that, despite how bad everything was, the goodness of the Lord prevails in the land of the living!

Now, when you talk about a church, what do you mean? A building? We may love the church buildings; they have associations and memories. But the church is decidedly not a building. The building just serves the convenience of the church. If our building were demolished, we could go to Central Park, into the meadow, and talk and think about Jesus Christ—and we would be the Church. It is not a building.

Nor is the church an institution, rigid and dogmatic, laying down certain rules. There may be some narrow-minded churches that do that, but not the real Church. This Church, at least, is not an institution, nor is it an ecclesiastical hierarchy. All churches have officers, boards, committees and the like, but there is great danger in the Church becoming a big machine. This Church is no machine. The real Christian Church is a group of people dedicated to Jesus

Christ, who said, "And ye shall know the truth, and the truth shall make you free" (John 8:32 KJV). We are a fellowship of people, excited people, released people, people who have been set free. We are common pilgrims together on the way that leads to truth—people committed to going out into society to do away with injustices and evils and build a better world in the name of Christ. We are a marching army, a group banded together, an alive fellowship.

I read an article based on interviews with college students around the country who said they were abandoning the Church. Their reasons: they were tired of dogmatism; they were tired of bombast; they were tired of institutionalism. Could it be that this is all there is to be found in some churches? God forgive us if that should be the case. This Church is a fellowship that is full of joy and happiness and ecstasy.

Some years ago a girl came here from the theatrical world and she was rather cynical and down on life, but she was hungry for something. She found it here in a group of people who had really had an experience of Jesus Christ. Her whole outlook changed and her face, good-looking before, became radiantly beautiful. A young man from her old sophisticated crowd asked, "What has happened to you? There's something about you . . ."

She tried as best she could to explain it to him, "I have Jesus Christ deep within me."

"I don't understand, but I know I want to marry you. Will you take me the way I am?" he asked.

"But that wouldn't be a very good marriage, would it? Let's just put it in God's hands and see."

They spent every possible moment together. He would bring her here to church, but would not come in, for he had the notion that

Christianity and the church were for women and old folk. He waited outside Sunday after Sunday. But he began to notice the people who came out of the church. More than half of them were men, and many were young men. They all seemed to be walking on air. He finally decided to go in, as he put it, to "see what goes on in this place."

She was a wise girl. She let him sit in a back pew until his resistance changed to interest. Then she brought him into the group that had made such a difference in her own life. (Ah, it's wonderful what a woman can do with a man when she has the touch of genius!) And his experience of Christ was even deeper. Today they live in a western state and their minister tells me they are one of the most powerful team influences in the whole area. What a change in their lives!

A long while ago I was pastor of a church upstate where I met a most remarkable human being, Harlowe B. Andrews. Everybody called him Brother Andrews. He was very religious, but he was very astute too. He is supposed to be the man who invented the first dishwasher. He also ran the first supermarket in the United States way back around 1890. He put perishable goods for sale on his shelves five days out of California by fast freight. He was a genius; never had much education, but he was a thinker. A banker in Syracuse told me he never knew a man who had such a gift for making money as Brother Andrews. He said, "All he has to do is put out his hand and money springs to him." I hung around him a long time trying to get the gift but never succeeded.

Well, the church there had a big debt. The Board had a meeting one night and decided they couldn't raise the whole debt—it was too much—but they would raise half the debt. I asked, "Where are we going to get it?"

"Why don't you go see Brother Andrews?" they suggested.

"You go!" I said.

"No," they insisted, "you go."

So I drove out to where Brother Andrews lived. I approached him very timorously, saying, "Brother Andrews, I just thought I'd come to see you."

He said, "I know that; you're here. But what do you want to see me about?"

"Well," I hesitated, "we must raise some money to try to clear off the church debt, Brother Andrews."

"How much are you going to raise?" he asked. I told him. He said, "That's only half the debt."

"Yes," I replied, "we didn't think we could raise more than half the debt."

"Well," he demanded, "what are you standing there looking at me for? What do you want me to do?"

"Are you going to give anything?" I asked.

"No," he said. "The answer is: not one nickel."

That didn't fill me with any burning enthusiasm, but I asked, "Why aren't you going to give?"

"Because you are only going to try raise half the debt for a great church of God. What is the matter with you?" Then he continued, "Let's get down on our knees and pray." It has been many years, but I still remember his prayer vividly. It went something like this: "Lord, this young fellow has been through a couple of schools and is supposed to be educated; but, You know, Lord, he just doesn't know anything. He hasn't got any nerve, and he is the poorest kind of religious leader You ever saw. He hasn't got the courage to ask anybody for money or to raise the whole debt." He paused and let a silence fall. Then he said, "Lord, if he will buck up and be a Christian and a real man and raise the whole debt, I'll give him five thousand dollars. Amen."

I stood up. "Are you actually going to give us five thousand dollars?" I asked with excitement.

"You heard what I told the Lord," he replied. "Five thousand dollars, if you raise the whole debt."

"But where are we going to get the rest of it?"

"Where you just got the first five thousand," he said. "You prayed for it and you got it."

"What do you know about that!" I exclaimed.

"Now you want to know where to go to get the rest of it, do you?"

"Yes."

"Well, get down on your knees again." This time he prayed, "Lord, please give us the name of a man who will give another five thousand dollars. Oh, thank You, Lord. I got the name. Thank You very much."

"Who is he?" I asked.

"It's Dr. So-and-So."

"Now look, Brother Andrews," I protested, "Dr. So-and-So is a sour, crabby man. He's a cynic. He hardly ever comes to church. And he is as tight as the bark on a tree. He'd never give us a nickel."

Brother Andrews reminded me, "I talked to the Lord, and the Lord told me you should go and ask him for five thousand dollars." And he added, "If he gives you five thousand dollars you'll be doing him the greatest favor anybody ever did him in his whole life. It will set him free from himself and give him happiness. Now go on down there and get that five thousand dollars."

As you can imagine, I drove very slowly. When I neared the medical building where the doctor had his office, I sort of hoped I wouldn't find a place to park. But right in front of the building I found one. There were three or four elderly ladies sitting in the waiting room. I told the nurse that I wanted to see the doctor, but since there were some people ahead of me, I would come back another day. "No," she said, "you can go on in."

I gulped. The doctor was sitting at his desk, a glum look on his face. He made a few discouraging remarks about life in general.

I thought, *Oh, the time isn't right.*

"All right, all right, Norman," he said, "what's the trouble with you? You're not sick, are you? Come on, come on. What is it you want?"

I began, "Well, we're raising some money . . ."

"Yes," he said, "I heard you were. All right. What do you want me to do? How much do you want me to give? Come on. Make it plain."

I looked at him and thought, *I wonder if he is good for a thousand dollars.* Then I got a vision of Brother Andrews's face. He is the kind of man upon whom you build nations and empires and kingdoms of God. His was a great face, like a granite cliff but a cliff against which the sun was shining. I shall never forget that wonderful man. I said to the doctor, "Look here, I'm your friend. I love you. I'm going to give you the greatest opportunity you ever had. I'm going to do you a tremendous favor. I'm going to let you give five thousand dollars."

"What's that?! Five thousand dollars!" And he mumbled in his beard. Finally he said, "All right. Something impels me to agree." And no sooner had he said it than he turned to his checkbook and wrote me a check for five thousand dollars.

Now that check proved to be a key that opened up to that man a whole new life. He got into the whole problem of the church debt with me. He became very enthusiastic. His entire personality changed. He lost his frustrations and fears. He became one of the most dynamic, released human beings I have ever known, and remained so until finally the Lord took him home one night into the heavenly Kingdom. He hit upon one of the greatest principles in man's experience: the release of life into joy and ecstasy by letting yourself go and giving your prayers, your money, and yourself.

So keep believing—never lose faith—and give as you've never given before; not just your money, but your heart. That is how to fill your life with abiding happiness.

NEW HEART WHEN DISHEARTENED

For God, who commanded the light to shine out
of darkness, hath shined in our hearts,
to give the light of the knowledge of the
glory of God in the face of Jesus Christ.

−2 Corinthians 4:6 KJV

Recently I had the privilege of addressing 1,500 students, candidates to be fliers in the United States Naval Air Force. This was at the United States Naval Air Training School at Pensacola, Florida. Following my talk, I met with the chaplains attached to that post. One of these chaplains had just returned from a year in Vietnam, and I asked him about his experience there. He said that he wouldn't have missed it for anything, but that it was a very harrowing time. He told of one particularly tough ordeal during a battle that raged across a small area for six hours or more. The shellfire was intense and went on for so long that it destroyed all vegetation between the opposing forces. A heavy rain had turned the ground into a sea of mud. The sky was dark and threatening. It was the chaplain's duty, or as he put it, "privilege" to go out and bring back the wounded men. This was done at great personal jeopardy, for the shellfire was heavy.

In this instance, crawling through the mud toward one man who was farther out than the rest, his strength suddenly left him. He was hit, superficially. He had already completed two or three errands of mercy, and now, flat on his stomach in the mud, his hands in the slime, the heart went completely out of him. He felt he could not go any farther.

"But just at that instant," he said, "there was a break in the clouds and a long shaft of sunlight came down to that muddy, bloody earth and moved across the end of carnage to a spot just in front of me and rested upon one beautiful lonely little flower growing up out of the muck. It was the only sign of vegetation left, a flower in the mud, surrounded by the dead and the dying, illuminated by a shaft of light. There came to me in that instant," he continued, "that passage of Scripture in 2 Corinthians where it says, 'For God, who commanded the light to shine out of darkness, hath shined in our hearts.' New heart came to me, an infusion of new strength filled my body, and a new determination made me know I could bring back that wounded man."

Now under less dramatic circumstances every one of us faces times and conditions in which our strength is depleted, our energy sapped, and we experience that deep trouble of the human spirit known as disheartenment. But just then, if you will look for it, God will repeat His miracle. He will cause "light to shine out of darkness" and you will have new heart when disheartened.

All over the world there are disheartened people. If you are not disheartened at this particular moment, by the law of averages you probably have been at some time, or you will be in the future. So it is very proper and wise and advantageous to know how to get new heart when you are disheartened.

One thing you can do is to deliberately and consciously build a backfire against disheartenment. When you're discouraged and gloomy, it is very hard to do anything constructive about it. The tendency is to wallow in gloom and get a kind of masochistic satisfaction. But if you do that, you are likely to remain in a gloomy, disheartened state. The person who really employs the principle of the backfire will find that he has great resources within himself and can rebuild his heart into happiness and optimism. I was reading the other day about the editor of a prominent American magazine who had been living a very tense, hectic life and finally, as a result, began feeling physically ill. The doctors did what they could to help him, prescribing medicine they thought would help. One doctor, however, told him that his trouble was depressiveness brought on by a hectic life.

Well, this editor, being a bright fellow, asked himself, *If I've been made ill by depressiveness, how can I make myself well?* And the answer was to start acting in the opposite way. If depressiveness had made him sick, then the opposite of depressiveness, he reasoned, would make him well. And he figured that the opposite of depressiveness was joy.

Now obviously he didn't *feel* joyful, but he *decided* that he would practice being joyful. He went out and bought every book he could find with an upbeat, satisfying, happy theme. He hunted up some TV presentations that were really funny, like *The*

Honeymooners (with Jackie Gleason). He invited to his home only friends who were good storytellers or good conversationalists. He didn't want anyone around saying, "I'm so sorry you're feeling depressed." He wanted those near him who had a real answer for their lives. Then, of course, he began to go deeper, turning to the One Who said, "These things have I spoken unto you . . . that your joy might be full" (John 15:11 KJV). Gradually, he began to build up against his depressiveness, deliberately, consciously, mentally, the great antidote of joy. This requires discipline. But he built a backfire against disheartenment.

And there is the case of a girl I knew in Youngstown, Ohio. She was a beautiful girl. She had a rich father. She had everything—good health, money, education. Then all of a sudden her father lost all his money. The family was reduced practically to poverty. And on top of that, her eyesight began to fail and presently she became totally blind. She went to every doctor she could find, and they all gave her the same diagnosis: there was no hope for her eye condition. Now here was a situation where a person had had everything and now she had nothing.

But that girl became one of the most radiant, creative human beings I have ever known. And how did she do it? She built a backfire against her trouble. She decided that if she couldn't see light, she would think light. So at frequent intervals each day she would stop and remember how light looked: how golden sunshine in the morning appeared, how light looked falling through the trees onto the grass or sparkling on a body of water. She thought constantly of light. Now this did not change the condition in the retina of her eyes, but it did change the attitude of her mind behind the eyes, so that it became full of light and she became one of the most dynamic personalities I ever met. She found new heart in her disheartenment.

The Bible just bubbles over with spiritual food for getting a new heart when disheartened. Dig in to the New Testament, and you come up with light and music and singing and health and hopefulness and faith and love. Your heart will begin to sing as you build a backfire against disheartenment. The shadows will flee away. So the next time you get disheartened say to yourself, *Okay, let's sit down and see how we can build a backfire.* This is for every-body, right from the Holy Scriptures. So think light, think health, think victory. Think good, not bad; think riches, not poverty. Think a backfire and build it. Light will shine in your darkness and give you a new heart when you are disheartened.

An important thing to realize about this is that it doesn't make any difference how much difficulty there is. Pile it as high as you want, make it just as big as you can, see it just as dark as possible—still there are always great possibilities in any situa-tion. Generally, when people are disheartened, they can't see the possibilities. They have shackles on their eyes. They see only the difficulties that are involved, not the solutions. The strange thing about human nature is . . . that we have a tendency to magnify the difficulties, to blow them up, to make them bigger than they actually are. The thing to do when you are disheartened is the very opposite: go hunting around in your situation for the bright possibilities that are surely there.

Oh, you may glare at me and say, "Now, look. I know! Don't give me any of that positive business. My situation is absolutely hopeless. I've had it. I'm up against a dead end." But I don't believe it at all. I've felt that way myself sometimes and then discovered that there were still possibilities. A man from Elmira, New York, called me on the telephone one afternoon and said, "I'm in an awful situation. I'm really at the end of my rope, and I am going to blow my brains out."

"Oh," I said to him, "I'm sorry you are going to blow your brains out. Why did you call me to tell me about it?"

"Well," he replied, "I thought you might have something to say to me before I do it."

"When are you going to blow your brains out?" I asked. "Do you have to do it today?"

"No," he answered, "I don't have to do it today. Why?"

"Well," I suggested, "could you get on a plane and come down to New York City? Let's have a talk before you do it. You can do it just as well down here as you can in Elmira."

I wasn't being flippant; I took it seriously. I didn't think he was going to blow his brains out, but you never can tell, you know. So I made an appointment, and the next day he came at the agreed time and sat down with me in my office. He put his head in his hands, and he said, "Everything is lost. It's hopeless. I'm walking in deep darkness."

I felt very sorry for the poor fellow. We had a prayer about it. Then I asked him, "Did you say everything was lost? Everything?"

"Yes, sir," he answered, "everything!"

"You mean to tell me there isn't one good thing you still have?"

"Not one," he asserted. "It's nothing but darkness. My troubles are piled as high as the sky, and there isn't one good thing left."

"Well, my friend," I said, "I would hate to disagree with you, but I'd like to explore this a little." I got out a big sheet of paper, drew a line down the middle, and headed one column, "Things I Have Lost," and the other, "Things I Still Have."

The man remarked, "You won't need that second column, because I have nothing left."

"Well," I persisted, "let me ask you a few questions. Your wife has left you, of course?"

"What do you mean, my wife has left me?" he retorted. "She wouldn't leave me. My wife loves me. She'd stick with me if everybody else turned against me. Of course she hasn't left me."

"That's great!" I said. "We'll put it in this second column. 'Item 1: Wife hasn't left me.'" Then I said, "No doubt your children are all in jail?"

"What are you driving at," he expostulated, "with such silly talk? My kids are good kids. Of course they're not in jail."

"Well," I reminded him, "you told me everything was lost. Yet your children aren't in jail. So let's put it down: 'Item 2: Children are not in jail.'" And I continued, "Most likely you can't eat. No appetite."

"You know," he replied, "it's a funny thing. As gloomy as I feel, I have a whale of an appetite. I can eat anything."

"And you don't get indigestion?"

"No, I have a cast-iron stomach."

So I wrote down: "Item 3: A cast-iron stomach."

And we went on through a few more things like that. Then I said, "Look at the things you've got left! Let's add them up." I drew a line under them and I said, "Plus God. Brother, you're in! What do you mean, you want to blow your brains out? All you need to do is blow your faith up."

Well, he sat there and stared at me. He said, "I wouldn't have believed it possible. Why did I have to spend all the time and money to come here from Elmira just to have you tell me what I should have known myself? I think I can handle things from here. Thank you a lot."

"Just be sure you realize," I said, "that I haven't even started the list of the blessings you have left."

It's a matter of your attitude of mind. What are you going to look for? The shadows? Or that bright sunlight that God commanded to shine out of darkness? If you are disheartened about anything today, forget it. Blow your faith up. Look to the bright and shining face of the Lord Jesus Christ. Let Him get into you and change your thinking. Start looking for all the marvelous possibilities you have.

In other words, get new heart. There is a verse in Psalm 51 that says, "Create in me a clean heart, O God" (verse 10 KJV). Can you get a new heart when you are old and tired and worn and weak and sick and discouraged? Of course you can. I'm not referring to the physical organ known as the heart. When we pray, "Create a new heart within me," what we are asking is for a new inner motivation, a new depth of feeling, new basic attitudes. We read continually these days about heart transplants, some of which succeed, some of which fail. But I can tell you of a heart transplant that never fails. It is when you come to the point where you commit your life to Jesus Christ and stop trying to run it yourself, many times making a mess of it, and ask Him to take it over. I have seen the most amazing, dramatic, fascinating, exciting changes in people who knew that they needed new heart, but couldn't get it themselves and who turned to the Lord Jesus Christ as their Savior and He saved them from themselves.

Recently at a place where I made a speech, a woman fairly bounded up to me as soon as I was through and grabbed me by the hand. I hadn't seen anybody with so much zip and energy in a very long while. She walked with a bounce; her most attractive face was alight; she was a beautiful woman. Yet I'm sure she wasn't a day under sixty according to the calendar. But in the quality of her actions she wasn't a day over twenty. She was vibrantly alive. She tried to tell me about herself—and I liked the way she did it. She had a good, clear, organized mind. She mentioned a series of heavy blows she had had, culminating in the death of her husband. She and her husband were devoted, she said—still in love after many years. "When he was gone," she said, "it was as though the whole world caved in on me. I wandered around in my gloom and self-pity for weeks on end, dragging myself around like an aged woman. All the life had gone out of me.

"Then one day," she continued, "I was reading about that transplant operation in South Africa where they took the heart of a young person and put it into an older person. And I thought to myself how great it would be if I could get a young heart—if I could have a heart like I had when I was sixteen, when I was so happy. But then I began to think; and the thought came to me that there was a Doctor who could give me the heart transplant I wanted, One who could renew the youth of any individual and enable him to 'mount up with wings as eagles.' So I just went to my knees, and went back to the Scriptures. I joined a small group in this city. And I found Him and He found me. He gave me a spiritual and mental heart transplant."

Whereupon she bounced out of the room like a dynamo. A man standing near me who had known the woman for some time shook his head, saying, "I would never have believed it possible that a person could be so transformed."

Now as this writing concludes, your same old problems are waiting for you. They are there, all right—you can count on that! But they are in for a surprise. They will hardly recognize you when you take them up again. They are going to say, "You are not the same person!"

And you can say, "No, I certainly am not, because now I'm building a backfire against disheartenment. I know there are possibilities for good in you, old problems, and I've had a heart transplant. What's more, the light has been commanded to shine out of darkness and I now walk in the light."

This can happen to you and to me and to all of us if we go forward with the Lord Jesus Christ.

ENTHUSIASM MAKES LIFE GOOD

The thief comes only to steal and kill
and destroy; I have come that they may
have life, and have it to the full.

–John 10:10 NIV

One of the greatest words in the English language is *enthusiasm*. It describes a spirit that adds zest to life. In fact, enthusiasm makes life good. It is a gift of God. The very word *enthusiasm* relates to God. It is derived from two Greek words, *en* and *theos*; *en* meaning "in" and *theos* being the Greek word for "God." So *enthusiasm* means in God or God-in-you; it means *full of God*.

Of course, the idea of enthusiasm isn't "in" with a certain segment of the American population today. For them enthusiasm is out; glumness is in. Enthusiasm is out; cynicism is in. But many of these bewildered souls will eventually discover to their sorrow that they are "out" by being "in," for enthusiasm does make life good.

How is your enthusiasm? Life with its buffetings may have knocked enthusiasm out of you. Or you may have become so sophisticated that you think enthusiasm is something that belongs to a bygone generation. Don't delude yourself. Get enthusiasm back. Without it life is poor; with it life is good. It makes you feel strong. It gives you a sense of mastery. It gives you a consciousness of your own value and worth. You take hold of the world when enthusiasm takes hold of you.

Enthusiasm, however, is a quality that must be affirmed and reaffirmed. My friend Donald Curtis, pastor of a church in Los Angeles, has a devotion that he suggests for daily use, and I think it's very good. He suggests you affirm to yourself each morning this or something equivalent to it: *I move serenely forward into the adventure of life today. I am filled with inspiration and enthusiasm. I am guided and protected by the Infinite in everything I say and do. I project confidence and authority. I am sure of myself in every situation. With God's help I am filled with the strength and energy to be what I am and to do what I have to do. . .*

That is the deep, rejuvenated consciousness you get when you let enthusiasm take over. Don't resist it. Don't reject it. Don't cast it out. Don't say you're too old for it. Don't say it isn't the "in" thing. Get in with this and you are really in.

The Christian religion is full of this. In the thirty-sixth Psalm, the ninth verse (KJV), are the words, "For with thee is the fountain of life." What a picture—the fountain of life! It brings to mind one glorious Sunday at the Palace of Versailles when all of a sudden they turned on the fountains and the water burst forth with a gush and a roar and an upthrust as though reaching for the sun, dancing and singing. "For with thee (God) is the fountain of life."

When you get God in your life, you get so excited that you can hardly endure it. It makes life good.

"I am come that they might have life," says that marvelous passage in the 10th chapter of John, "and that they might have it more abundantly" (verse 10 KJV). Or, as the New Century Version has it: "I came to give life—life in all its fullness." You see, Christianity is designed to produce not glum, sour, growling, griping people, but happy people, lilting people, victorious people, enthusiastic people. All this takes into account the pain and problems in the world. Despite problems, and even out of them, God brings to people a consciousness and plan of victory.

Enthusiasm makes life good. The enthusiast has enormous resources, so great that they will equate with any problems he ever has to face. This doesn't mean that the enthusiast won't fail. He will fail. Everybody will fail at times. Failure is a common experience of all mankind. You're going to fail sometimes. So am I. Many times. But that is not the crux of the story. It is *how* you fail. The enthusiast fails, but he "fails forward," and that is a great way to fail. In fact, it's a good thing to fail if you fail forward. That phrase "fail forward" isn't my own. I got it from a man whom I used to know, whom I consider one of the wisest born philosophers this country ever had—Charles F. Kettering. He was for many years the chief research scientist of General Motors Corporation. He developed the self-starter, the Duco paint process, high-octane gasoline, and many other refinements in the automotive field. Next to Edison, he was perhaps the finest inventive mind we've had in modern times. He was a natural thinker. He thought great thoughts. And one of his thoughts was this idea of "failing forward."

He used to say that as a research scientist, he had failed many times, but from each failure he had learned something—always "failing forward" toward the day when some later experiment would be successful. It may take many failures to prepare you for a success, so you should never fail and stop, but fail forward.

Years ago I heard Julius Rosenwald, who at that time was president of Sears, Roebuck and Co., quote this saying: "If life hands you a lemon, make lemonade of it." In other words, fail forward with it. Don't let your problems overwhelm you.

There are always people saying that the times are against them and that this is no time to imagine you can live a satisfying life, with conditions in the world as they are today. Isn't it strange that there are always people running down the time in which we live as if every other time were perfect? Well, the enthusiast rises above all such miserable thinking. There have always been some people who took the time they lived in just the way it was and with enthusiasm made something of it. The best time is really right this minute. How do you know how many more minutes you are going to have, anyway? This is it. Emerson said, "Everyone is criticizing and belittling the times. Yet I think that our times, like all times, are very good times, if only we know what to do with them."

It really is pathetic that so many people today, especially young people, are so sad because they feel that there is something terribly wrong with the world now. There is plenty wrong with the world, and there is plenty wrong with what the present generation of radical intellectuals call the establishment, and there is also plenty wrong with those who don't like the establishment— so there you have it: there's something wrong with everybody and everything. But we still can keep in mind what is right with things. A few years ago on California Street in San Francisco, a sour-looking intellectual whom I had never met walked up and spoke to me. How did I know that he was an intellectual? He told me he was. Well, he looked at me sourly and said, "I'm glad to meet you. You're the bright Pollyanna-ish, sweetness-and-light individual who runs around the country talking about positive thinking, aren't you?"

"I do go around talking about positive thinking," I replied, "which is neither Pollyanna-ish nor sweetness and light. I'll tell you what a positive thinker is, son, if you're interested to know. A positive thinker is a man who is tough enough mentally so that he sees all the difficulties in this life, but sees them straight, and having a knowledge of Almighty God, knows what he himself is and knows that he is equal to any problem he will ever have to face."

The man countered, "But don't you know that the world is full of problems?"

"You don't say?" I said. "You think I was born yesterday? Of course the world is full of problems." But then I thought of a come-back and I've been proud of myself ever since. Most of my come-backs come back about six hours after I actually need them! I said, "Certainly the world is full of problems, but thanks be to God, it is also full of the overcoming of problems."

That really got him. He went off down the street shaking his head, and I could hear it rattle all the way down the block.

Of course the world is full of problems. It always has been; it always will be; it is now. But those who know God, who know the Lord Jesus Christ, can affirm, "For with thee (despite these problems) is the fountain of life." And they are the kind of people who get the problems solved. Last September my wife decided that she and I should go to the Mayo Clinic for a checkup. I don't know where she got this idea. It didn't appeal to me. I said, "There's nothing wrong with me, except maybe my mind is weak." To which she readily agreed. I said, "Forget it. I'm not going." So what do you think happened? We went! We went through three days of examinations and we both came out 100 percent: they gave us a wonderful bill of health—and of course we were very happy about it.

As we were leaving, we encountered in an elevator a couple who recognized me and spoke to us. I asked the man, "Have you been through the clinic?"

"Yes, I have."

"I hope you had good news," I said.

"No," he replied, "I didn't. I've got to stay over for more biopsies." And, with an expression on his face that was pathetic, he added, "Dr. Peale, I'm afraid."

His wife, putting her arm around him, said, "Honey, you don't need to be afraid; you're going to be all right."

"I know," he said, "but I'm afraid."

Well, I was so touched I couldn't help loving the man, and I put my hand on his shoulder. I could actually feel him tremble. Now, what would you say to a person under those circumstances? I didn't know what to say. But I asked God what to say, and He helped me. "Look, let me tell you something. God loves you. He really does. You just put yourself in His hands. Rest yourself in His love."

With that, the tears came to his eyes, and he grabbed me by the hand and said, "You'll never know what that does to me."

And God loves you too. Rest on that love and you won't need to be afraid of anything.

Now a lot of people think of enthusiasm as something volatile and hot. The enthusiast according to caricature is a noisy, superficial, hotheaded individual. Well, there is fire in the enthusiast, all right, but in the true enthusiast it is fire under control. The English writer William McFee said, "The world belongs to the enthusiast who keeps cool." Keep your enthusiasms, but keep them under control. Don't let them freeze, keep the motivation under them, but keep them controlled. Then there isn't any knot that you can't disentangle.

I know a man who fits this description perfectly. He is a successful individual who has had many hard blows and difficulties in his life. He's had success, he's had failure. And he's a thinker. He knows the resources of life and where they are to be found. He is an enthusiast and he has cool, collected control. I asked him one time to tell me why nothing ever seems to upset him. He said it was due to using five words to keep himself under control. Here is what he said (I wrote it down): "I work enthusiastically. I take success gratefully. I receive failure dynamically. (That means taking it without getting all distressed and excited about it. It means that when you fail, you take it in your stride and keep proceeding forward.) I deal with people and situations philosophically. I keep an attitude toward life positively." So there are the five good words: *enthusiastically, gratefully, dynamically, philosophically, positively.*

Did it ever occur to you that life is not some thing that you just muddle through without following any rules? The kind of living that makes life good is a science. Life responds to certain definite methods and procedures. Your life can either be a miss or be a hit, can either be empty or be full, depending on how you proceed with it. And the enthusiast, first, knows and draws upon the resources. Second, he plays it cool and straight. Finally, he believes there is nothing in life so difficult that it can't be overcome. And with faith in God and in the Lord Jesus Christ, that is a fact. This faith can move mountains. It can change people. It can change situations. It can change the world. If you get it in you, you can overcome all the great storms in your life.

Life is full of storms. You may be living in halcyon days right now. Don't let that fool you; it can't always be that way. It was never designed to be that way. "Man is born unto trouble, as the sparks fly upward," says the fifth chapter of Job (verse 7 KJV). You will encounter storms. Do you feel equipped? Can you handle them, or will they beat you down? Storms of life come when least expected. Sunshine, rain, fog, mist, storms; sunshine, rain, fog, mist, storms—so it goes. Well, the enthusiast knows that he has, by the gift of God and through the Lord Jesus Christ, the power to ride out the storms. Let me tell you of one incident. Recently my wife and I were sitting on a plane when the stewardess came and asked my name. When I told her she said, "The pilot says he knows you, and he wants you to come up to the cockpit and have a visit with him." This was an interesting invitation, so I went up to the cockpit. The pilot told the copilot he could go out for a while, and I sat in the copilot's seat. Very informal kind of plane—there weren't as many regulations governing commuter routes in those days.

This pilot was a long, lanky Texan. He said, "I heard you were aboard, and I want to talk with you about religion." That was his beginning. I was surprised, but pleased and interested. "I want to thank you," he continued. "You helped me find Jesus Christ, and ever since then my life has been altogether different." And we talked of spiritual things.

Then I got interested in the plane and in all the gadgets he had there. I asked, "Are these planes hard to run?"

"No," he said, "any fool can do it. Want to try?"

"Well," I responded, "what do I do?"

"You take hold of this stick," he said, "and keep your eye on that level. You must keep the plane on that level." And he showed me how. And I sat there flying this plane through the big, expansive sky. However, I saw out of the corner of my eye that the pilot had his hand on the other stick.

Presently I saw two great big cumulus clouds sitting out there ahead, with a path of blue between them. I asked, "Do you want me to go around those clouds or through them?"

"Go through," he replied.

So we went straight through, with the clouds reaching for us on either side. It was so thrilling that I exclaimed, "Boy, that was great! Let's go around and come through again, what do you say?"

"Better just keep on going," he said. "We'll be on the Tokyo radar in a minute and they'd be wondering what's going on out here."

Then he took it away from me. I had read in the paper that the typhoon season was approaching, and I asked, "What would you do if we suddenly ran into a typhoon?"

He answered, "I wouldn't run into one if I had my wits about me. You don't want to fool around with a typhoon. What I try to do when there's a typhoon around is get on the edge of it, the way it's traveling. Usually it measures from three to five hundred miles across. The thing to do is find out which way it is moving and get on the edge of it so that it blows you ahead." Then he cast off a phrase that I thought was a classic. "You turn typhoons into tailwinds."

A person who lives with the Lord Jesus Christ, and therefore has enthusiasm and calm control, does the same with the storms of life. He lets them take him to higher ground. He turns typhoons into tailwinds. Enthusiasm makes life good.

LIFE CAN BE FULL OF MEANING

Ask and it will be given to you; seek and you will
find; knock and the door will be opened to you.

–Matthew 7:7 NIV

For many years I have emphasized one repetitive theme. It is that life can be absolutely wonderful, that anybody can gain victory over himself and all the circumstances of this life, that a person can live with joy and zest and enthusiasm, that he can put himself up against this troubled world and infuse it with new life, and that all of this can be done not by a person's own strength, but through the power of Jesus Christ in his heart.

So often today we hear people moaning that life has no meaning. How any enlightened, intelligent, perceptive individual could decry this marvelous thing called life and say that it has no meaning is to me beyond all comprehension! Yet today we hear thousands of young people growling and grumbling that there is no meaning in life.

What is the matter with them? Can't they see? Can't they receive? Can't they feel? Have they no depth of understanding?

You can have a life full of meaning if you fill it full of meaning. Your life can be wonderful if you see the wonder in it. Your life can be full of interest if you take an interest in it. Your life can be exciting if you live and think excitedly. You can do anything you want with your life if you will do it. You can take hold of it and shape it and make it meaningful.

I'm going to say something here that might seem counterintuitive at first: the thing that makes life is its problems. If a person doesn't like what goes on, why doesn't he take hold of it, do something about it, make it the way it ought to be? Life is a tremendous thing if you get a creative attitude toward it. A friend of mine, for example, began to fall on gloomy days. His mind was full of darkness. He had made a few mistakes, he had messed things up, and he was deeply unhappy. The zest for life had left him. One day he met another friend of mine, an older man, for dinner in a restaurant on East 61st Street in Manhattan. The older man was Smiley Blanton, the psychiatrist, my dear friend and associate for over thirty years and one of the wisest human beings I ever knew. Smiley was a character. He wore a sloppy hat jammed down on his head. I could never understand how a man could wear such an awful-looking hat. But that hat was really a part of Smiley. He also wore an old, beat-up raincoat, which he used to pull up around his ears. He was a genius in understanding human beings.

Well, Smiley met my unhappy younger friend and, being quick to feel the mental condition of another individual, he asked, "What's wrong, young man?"

So the younger man began to pour out his misery, frequently interjecting, "If only I hadn't done that!" "If only I had handled this thing better!" "If only I had foreseen the way it was going to turn out!" For fifteen minutes this gloomy "if only" recital went on. The poor man had lost all sense of the meaning of life.

Finally the doctor said, "Come over to my office. I want you to listen to a tape recording of three unidentified people talking to me about themselves." For maybe a half an hour he listened to three miserable human beings declaring how bleak life was. Then Dr. Blanton asked him, "What two words did you find embedded in the talk of all three of these people?"

The young man answered, "They seemed to keep saying, 'If only I hadn't done this . . .' 'If only I had done that . . .' 'If only it hadn't turned out that way . . .' 'If only . . .'"

The old psychiatrist said, "You have spoken the saddest two words in the English language. If only! If only."

"Well," asked the young man, "what do I do?"

And the wise old man replied, "You must substitute for those two sad words two creative words. I tell you what: Eject those two words—*if only*—out of your mind and put instead the two words: 'Next time.'"

My younger friend told me later, "I tried those two words: next time. I liked them. I slid them into my mind and could almost hear them click fast. And my life was changed. It was really remarkable. When any discouragement came, I found myself saying, 'With the help of Jesus Christ, next time!'"

Everyone has his times of failure, of defeat, of frustration; but no defeat or failure or frustration is permanent. There is always a next time! Life is good. I wonder why the Lord brings the dawn around every twenty-four hours. It should remind us that though the night is black, there can still be a new day. So live with the attitude of *next time*.

That is one secret of making life meaningful. And a second is to practice the great principle that you can if you think you can. There isn't any good thing you cannot do if you will think you can. There is my esteemed friend W. Clement Stone. He is a very successful businessman. Through extraordinary intelligence, hard work, and the application of the basic laws of successful achievement, he has made huge sums of money. But he gives it away under the equally important laws of benevolent motivation and always for creatively human purposes and values. He has given over a million dollars to various charities. I never knew a man who gave so much money so generously as does Mr. Stone. It appears that his chief reason for making money is to help people. For example, he has helped more prisoners to find new life—and more boys to find a future—than anybody I know. He started life with nothing. He was utterly poverty-stricken. He said that the Lord just gave him the gift of making money.

But I've noticed that a lot of people who make money hang on to it. Some of the tightest people I've ever known are people who have made money—they've got the idea that it is for them alone. If you have the ability to acquire wealth, you should learn the equally important art of how to give it for mankind. You are a steward of God, Who made everything and owns all values of this world.

Mr. Stone is a philosopher who says you should read the Bible with the idea that God wants to do wonderful things for you. You get exactly what you are looking for, he says. If you seek inspiration, you become inspired. If you seek knowledge, you become informed. If you seek wisdom, you become wise. If you seek health, sickness disappears. Seek good, and it comes to you. Seek success, and it will come to you. Know specifically what you want and then keep your mind on that which you want and off the things you don't want. If you keep thinking about what you don't want, you'll get what you don't want. But if you think about what you want, it is likely to come to you.

Mr. Stone declares that the greatest, most creative text is Matthew 7:7 (KJV): "Ask, and it shall be given you; seek, and ye shall find; knock, and it shall be opened unto you." And he paraphrases it: "Ask for the specific thing that you desire. Believe, put it in God's hands, and if it is His will, you will receive it."

Then look for it. Get into action. Think creatively. What do you want out of life? You can if you think you can! There are so many depressed people in the world today talking about how American society is going to pieces and saying that the younger generation doesn't amount to anything. The younger generation is all right; it is just the way they have been handled that is the problem, or the way they are handling themselves, some of them. I was reading about Archie Moore. Well, Archie Moore is a former champion prize fighter, a big, husky man. Not long ago he was given an award as "Mr. San Diego"—the leading citizen of San Diego. He is a great Christian. Three or four years ago, he became worried about the vandalism at the hands of boys in the lowest-income section of a smaller California town. So he thought he would try to help these boys, and he began pondering how to do it.

He put up a punching bag outdoors in the street and stood there punching this bag. A little boy came up wide-eyed and looked at him and said, "Gee, mister, you sure do know how to punch that bag!" He added, "You know something? I can do it the same as you."

"You can, eh?" said Archie. "Tell you what you do. You bring ten more kids here tomorrow. I want to see how good you all do it."

Next day the little boy showed up not with ten other kids—but with thirty kids. Archie asked them, "You boys want to learn to fight?"

"Yeah, we want to learn to fight."

"Well," he said, "then you've got to learn the ABCs of fighting. Remember that the A comes before the B and the B comes before the C. The first thing you've got to do is to learn defense. You've got to learn to shadowbox. And you never want to learn to fight in order to hurt anybody; you want to learn to fight so that when a bully attacks, you know you are strong and can walk away from him in dignity."

He was giving them instruction in right living, you see, while he taught them to use the punching bag. And pretty soon he was teaching not thirty kids but sixty kids. One day he said, "Boys, what do you say we start a club?" They all wanted to join. And Archie Moore called it the ABC Club—ABC for Any Boy Can. One of the rules was that each day when the program started every boy had to show his school report card or graded test. If a boy's grades weren't good enough, he got thrown out until he got them up to snuff. The local schoolteachers were astonished at the new high grades made by kids who previously had been scraping the bottom. And this led to Moore's developing a similar program on a larger scale in San Diego, where he lives.

A meeting of ABCs comes to order when Archie calls out, "Students!" The boys fall into line and recite the Pledge of

Allegiance, smartly placing their saluting arms across their hearts: "I pledge allegiance to the flag of the United States of America and to the republic for which it stands, one nation, under God, indivisible, with liberty and justice for all."

Then Archie Moore calls out the question, "What does ABC mean?"

The boys shout with one voice: "Any Boy Can—if he wants to."

"If he wants to what?"

"Wants to improve himself," they shout, "and be a better student and a better American."

"What can a good student become?"

"Doctor!" "Preacher!" "Actor!" "Governor!" "President!"

And Archie Moore asks, "What does a good student not do?"

And the answers are: "He doesn't steal. He doesn't drink. He doesn't do drugs."

Boys out of the ghetto, black and white, rise to higher ways of living because of the influence of a godly prize fighter who teaches them a basic principle: Any Boy Can If He Thinks He Can. This country is not going down the drain, friends. Not while it has Archie Moores who love their fellow men and who teach so astutely the great principle: You Can If You Think You Can. Life can be full of meaning if you know what to do about the hard things, because it is the hard things that knock the life out of you. These hard things aren't very pleasant, but they are awfully good for us. We aren't supposed to go through life on flowery beds of ease. Whoever masters the tough becomes tough, and when he becomes tough he finds meaning.

A couple, members of Marble Collegiate Church, was recently robbed. Someone broke the lock on their door, messed up their apartment, and took all the valuables they most highly prized. They have illness in the family too. It must have been quite a shock to them that in the supposedly protected apartment house where they live, such a thing could happen. But it doesn't seem to have shaken their serenity. I asked them, "Why are you so calm about it?"

The man answered, "Well, you know, it just proves that God must like us and knows we can handle problems. He has given us such a mess of them at one time."

Now that is what I call spiritual maturity. They don't expect life to be easy; they just take it as it comes and relate it to God, happy that He likes them so much that He trusts them with many problems.

All around us in this world there are people who are in trouble, in need, in sorrow, in poverty, in sickness, in unhappiness, in misery. If you want to make life meaningful for yourself, get out and do something about it. Get into it. Get out of your comfortable ways. People who find meaning in life are people who give themselves for other people and get into hard things in the world. Like a Mexican migrant worker I heard about. I suppose when you get right down to it, one of the most underprivileged groups of people in this country is the migrant farm laborer. Many of them don't speak English. They follow the crops and live in a very unfortunate, economically depressed manner. They just don't belong anywhere. It is one of the groups in this country that is really neglected. Some of the churches have been trying to do something for the migrants, but it is not enough. For too many people they are still just statistics— migrant workers. Well, one of these workers is named Manuel Corral. And he did a heroic thing. Afterward at the Adolphus Hotel in Dallas they gave a big banquet in his honor. The hall was filled with people paying tribute to a little Mexican worker who can't speak English. And as he sat there at the head table a little boy named Randy McKinley, three years old, came running to him and climbed up on Manuel's knee and put his arms around Manuel's neck, put his head down on Manuel's shoulder—and went to sleep. When Manuel rose to receive his award, the little boy still clung to his neck, his blond curls against the Mexican's dark hair.

The story is this: One day Randy, age three and very slight, was running around in the yard of his grandparents' Texas farmhouse. Somebody had removed a barrel that had been placed over the top of an old abandoned well cased with a sixteen-inch pipe. Happy little Randy stepped into this open space and disappeared into the pipe— which went down three hundred feet, with the water level sixty-eight feet below the ground! The other children cried out in terror and ran to Randy's mother, and she ran to the well and put her arm down into the pipe—but her hand encountered nothing and she could hear displaced pebbles bouncing off down into the deep, dark distance. She screamed again and again: "Randy! Randy!" Faintly from below she heard a little voice that told her that he was alive.

She began screaming for help. Manuel Corral happened to be working in a field nearby, with three other men. The four came running. Manuel, though he couldn't understand a word of English, knew at once what had happened. He told the others to make a long, strong line from pieces of rope and baling wire. Then he had them tie it around his ankles and lower him headfirst into the pipe.

The pipe was sixteen inches in diameter, and Manuel, although he weighed only 125 pounds, was seventeen inches across the shoulders. But by hunching his shoulders he was able to get through the opening. And down he went into the darkness. The air in the long-unused well was foul-smelling. Noxious gases made him feel deathly sick. But he pushed on down the pipe for twenty feet until he came to an inverted *Y*, where the shaft branched and went two ways. Which way should he go? He sent up a prayer asking, "*Dios* (God), tell me which!" He took one of the shafts and went on down, down into the blackness, getting stuck every few feet, forcing his way on, realizing he could not stay conscious much longer in his head-down position. He could feel his skin scraping off against the pipe.

But finally his groping hand felt a tousled, wet head of hair, and he could hear the sound of a child gasping and choking. The boy was clinging to a narrow ledge just below the waterline. Manuel locked his arms under the child's armpits and cried out to the men to pull up fast. They started to pull. But the way he was holding the child had wedged Manuel's shoulders against the pipe so that they stuck. For a moment he had the awful, terrorized feeling that he was going to die there head downward in a pipe so many feet below the ground.

But gradually they pulled them up. Manuel could feel his shoulder sockets being dislocated. He was bloody and sick, and his head was injured. Once out of the well, he just lay on the grass while the mother hugged her little child, murmuring, "Oh, thank God, thank God!" The people standing around took up a collection and offered the brave Mexican one hundred dollars in gratitude, but he refused it. He shook his head, pointing up, and just said, "*Dios.*" For God.

"Ask, and it shall be given you; seek, and ye shall find; knock, and it shall be opened unto you" (KJV). Believe that you can and you can . . . Give yourself to the hard, tough problems in this world. And life will be full of meaning.

WHY WORRY WHEN YOU CAN PRAY?

I sought the Lord, and he answered me;
he delivered me from all my fears.
—Psalm 34:4 NIV

The title of this piece was suggested by a circus clown who happens to be a friend of mine. Being a clown is a serious business, and this particular clown is said to be one of the best men in his profession. His name is "Happy" Kellems.

"Happy" often writes to me, and I like his letters. He usually encloses a check for the work of the church. But more important than that, he gives witness to his faith. Now and then he will telephone me from some city where he is entertaining, and not long ago we had a conversation that ran something like this:

"How are you, Happy?"

"Oh, I'm getting along all right, with the Lord's help."

"Are things going well?" I asked.

"Well, you know how it is. We all have our ups and downs, the bitter with the sweet."

"I hope you're not worrying about things."

"Of course not," he replied. "Why worry when you can pray?" This struck me! It is a very sound philosophy toward this tragic tendency known as worry or anxiety.

In fact, the best way to handle worry is to subject it to prayer. It cannot continue to exist in the mind of an individual who prays in depth. Prayer-in-depth cancels out worry. Somebody said to me this morning, "You have a good title for your sermon." I replied that I hoped the sermon would be as good as the title. But if the sermon does not measure up, I tell you what you do: You just say to yourself every day, "Why worry when you can pray?" And in due course you will get your worry under control.

Sometimes when you lift a subject like worry into the pulpit, people wonder a bit. The reaction might be that the pulpit is a place for the discussion of more profound problems than that of worry; instead, some great philosophical, sociological, theological matter ought to be the subject of the sermon. I'll agree to the importance of preaching on such themes. But I will also insist that the function and purpose of the pulpit is to help people. Jesus Christ went about doing good. He loved people. He put His hand of healing upon them. He always helped people. You can take the great truths He spoke and apply them to the very complex problems of the day. But when you come right down to it, what could possibly be more complex in its effect both upon individuals and upon people in the mass than this insidious thing called worry?

Let me illustrate the importance of this problem by telling of an incident that occurred recently. I went to Wisconsin to give a talk at a United Fund affair. My host, who is the head of a large firm, sent his company plane to take me to his city. I have never had such a ride, though I have been on small planes a good many times. This one was a Learjet. On this model only four people can be accommodated, beside the pilots. On takeoff it fairly shoots into the sky. The nearest analogy in describing it is to say it is like a bullet. It races for the high places. I was delighted. I remarked to the pilot that I thought I ought to have one of them myself. He asked, "Why don't you buy one—on some easy monthly payment basis?"

"What is the price?" I asked.

"A million dollars," he replied. I decided I wouldn't get one.

We cruised at 45,000 feet. I said to the pilot, "This is the nearest to heaven I've ever been in my life." And then it occurred to me that that is no kind of discussion to have at 45,000 feet. You could see the curvature of the earth. It was an exalted, uplifting experience—quite smooth, like a leaf wafting through infinite space. The next day the gentleman who owns the plane took us on to Des Moines. This time we only got up to 41,000 feet.

Well, on this trip I fell to talking with our host—a remarkable man, highly educated, a deeply dedicated Christian, a man of profound thoughtfulness, a scholar in business, you might say, who has helped many people and who understands, too, how to help them. He is a very composed kind of man, and in the course of our conversation, I asked, "Do you ever have trouble with worry?"

"No," said he, "not anymore."

"What do you mean, 'not anymore'?" I asked.

"I would not worry for anything in this world," he replied, "because I once experienced the devastating damage worry can do to a human being. I wouldn't trifle with it at all." He then told me that some years ago he loaned some men a large sum of money for an enterprise that he thought they would manage successfully. He expected to have a part in the guidance of it, as well as a share of the profits. However, he soon became aware that these men weren't capable of good management. But they took control of the enterprise and in effect forced him out, as far as exercising any jurisdiction was concerned. Presently he developed a bad case of bronchitis, so bad that he had to sit up at night, unable to sleep, racked by deep coughs, and feeling that his throat was being strangled. He consulted a doctor, he took medication, but with little effect. "Finally," he said, "I came to the conclusion that it must be worry plus resentment that was causing this terrible bronchitis and choking."

When he had twice mentioned choking, I reminded him that the original meaning of the word *worry* is "to choke or strangle." He looked at me in surprise and said, "You don't say! Well, I came to that independently. And I knew I had to do something about it. I prayed until I was able to forgive everybody. Then I prayed until I got to the point where I was willing to put the whole matter, together with the people, in the hands of God and let it go."

The final outcome, he told me, was not what he had hoped, but it was satisfactory. The big thing was that the minute he ceased worrying and resenting, his physical condition began to improve, until finally the bronchitis cleared up entirely and he choked no more. He repeated, "I would be afraid to worry."

The damaging effect of worry does not always manifest so radically as in this case. But if you are inhibited in your life, if things don't go right, if you don't feel right, if you haven't got a grasp on things, just maybe it would be a good idea to examine the extent and depth of worry and anxiety in your mental and emotional condition.

How, then, is worry dispelled by prayer? There is a passage in the thirty-fourth Psalm that is a wonderful one. I suggest you commit it to memory and use it often. It goes like this: "I sought the Lord, and he heard me, and delivered me from all my fears" (verse 4 KJV). What a statement! You seek the Lord, He hears you, and He delivers you. From a few of your fears? No, from *all* your fears. So, why worry when you can pray? It is either, or. You can worry, or you can pray and have no worry.

Now just what does the process of praying do to you that relieves you of worry? One thing it does is release and activate your built-in strength. Every one of us has more strength by far than he ever dreamed of. Have you ever used all your strength? All of it? No, you have never used one-half of your strength, nor have I. I'll go further and say that I doubt that any of us has ever used one-tenth of his strength. We have tremendous reservoirs of power that we could call into action if we would. You can prove that to yourself by considering things that people do under crisis. Most astonishing things are done in crisis.

Like what happened once when a truck fell over onto a young boy. We had an article about it in *Guideposts*. The crowd was trying to lift the truck off of him. For some reason their combined efforts could not do it. Along came a fair-sized man—not a big man—a fair-sized man. He saw the situation. He never said a word. He crouched down, put his shoulders under the truck, and lifted it with just enough force for the boy to be pulled free. Later, they asked him to lift it again, to show how he had done it. He couldn't budge it.

Why could he do it the first time and not the second? Because the second time there was no crisis to activate the necessary strength. And what strength had been activated the first time? Was it strength outside of him? Of course not. It was inside of him—and it came out when it was needed. I wouldn't know but the greatest achievement in life is to know how to break out from yourself continually the strength that is there. You pray the strength out, you believe it out, you practice it out. And then the worry fades away. It is amazing the strength that people have—that you have and I have. Why, then, should we go crawling through our days afraid of life? Worrying about it?

I clipped an article out of the *Des Moines Register* the other day. If you read newspapers all the way through, you will sometimes find great human stories. This one was about a twenty-eight-year-old pilot who was flying a little pontoon plane up in northwestern Ontario. He was scouting an isolated little lake, far from civilization— nobody around anywhere for miles. And he set this little plane down on pontoons. He stepped out of the cockpit onto one of the pontoons to go about his business. The propeller was still turning. He slipped, hitting his head, and toppled unconscious into the water. Apparently the cold water revived him, and he came to, got hold of a pontoon, and tried to haul himself onto it. Then he discovered to his horror that the propeller had cut his right arm off slightly below the shoulder and he was bleeding profusely.

So there he is: far from civilization, in a lake, arm cut off, his lifeblood coursing out. What would you do? Worry? That sure would help you a great deal, wouldn't it! What did he do? He prayed. And he got an answer. He managed to pull himself up onto the pontoon and into the cockpit. He succeeded in fastening a tourniquet around the bleeding stump. He did what was necessary to lift the plane off the water into a beautiful takeoff. Praying all the while that he would not black out, he flew it fifteen miles and landed on another lake, where another pilot took over and flew him to Port Arthur and got him to the hospital. His life was saved, even though his arm was gone.

The newspaper commented that everyone was astonished by the incredible power that this man had over himself. He is a man of prayer, and he found that prayer gave him power; whereas worry, in that crisis, would have destroyed him. God spare us from ever undergoing an ordeal like that one! But in one degree or another, every last one of us has faced situations that, because of their importance to us individually, needed all the power we could summon. Don't you ever say to yourself, *I can't handle it.* You can handle anything. With God you are greater than you think. Believe it. It's the truth. "I sought the Lord, and he heard me . . ." He always will. ". . . and (He) delivered me from all my fears." Not a few of them, *all* of them. So why worry when you can pray? A second thing that prayer teaches is to think—and that, too, eliminates worry. One of the greatest things a human being can do is to think. So many of us don't. You ought to try it sometime. Really amazing things happen. God gave us this tremendous power, the ability to think, and when you think God's thoughts after Him, you are operating on God's wavelength. Praying activates the mind, so that you understand, you perceive, you get increased know-how, you become more alert, more in tune with ultimate wisdom and therefore ultimate power.

When a person worries, he has a nice little accompanying disease. These two go together, like Siamese twins. When you see one of them, look for the other and you will see it. They are inseparable. When you have worry, you have tension; when you have tension, you have worry. I can't remember anybody who was a worrier who wasn't also a victim of tension. Worry is like a shivering; it agitates the mind so that deeper knowledge cannot come up from the unconscious depths, because the surface of the mind is disturbed by this tension. When you pray, you become calm and serene and confident. You have tranquility and therefore tension dies. This leaves worry alone and it withers on the vine. Pray tension away and in the same process you pray worry away. When you are free from tension and your mind is operative, there isn't anything you can't handle.

In the 1968 World Series there was a great demonstration of this. A pitcher by the name of Mickey Lolich was pitching for the Detroit Tigers in the seventh game. Now this man had wanted to pitch in the World Series for years. The Tigers hadn't won the championship since 1945. They wanted to win this World Series. So they fought along until they and the St. Louis Cardinals had each won three games and they got into this seventh game. When the Cardinals came to bat in the last half of the ninth inning, the Tigers were ahead, 4–0. Mickey Lolich, pitching his third game in this Series, had the prize in his view.

He got the first man out. He got the second man out. He only had one out now between himself and athletic immortality. But along came a problem. The third man at bat didn't act right. He didn't cooperate. He hit one right over the barrier—a home run. So Lolich's shut-out went out the window. But he still had a three-run lead. In that moment, the manager of his team walked out to the mound for one of those mysterious conversations.

In the stands, 55,000 people sat spellbound. Were they going to take him out, just when he had this victory in his grasp? But they didn't take him out.

I happened to see a television interview with Mickey Lolich that night. The interviewer asked, "Mickey, when the manager came out to the mound, what did he say?" Well, as Mickey then related it, the mysterious conversation had gone something like this:

"Mickey, you are a little tense, aren't you, boy?"

"Yes, sir, I feel a little steamed up."

"You are worrying that maybe they'll get to you, they'll start hitting you, and we'll lose this game and lose this prize? Isn't that it?"

"Yes, sir."

"Look, boy, that worry is making you tense, and that tension can throw off your timing. I tell you what I want you to do. Remember when you first started playing baseball and you used to pitch on vacant lots? Remember you had the time of your life? Remember all those afternoons this past summer when you weren't pitching in the World Series—you were pitching in regular baseball games and you loved it?"

"Yes, sir," Lolich answered.

"All right," said the manager, "just forget the prize of the World Series and pitch because you love it."

So Mickey took a long look at the next batter. He wound up and pitched the ball not over the corner of the plate, but right down the middle with a little hook curve. The batter connected with it, but on the edge, and the ball went into the air in a pop-fly. The catcher caught it, and the game and the series were over.

Now, I wish I could tell you the manager had said to him to pray about it. That would have made my illustration perfect. But he didn't say that. However, the point is that praying is the surest of all ways to get back to calmness and tranquility of mind. And when you remain so, worry abates and your natural skills will be operating. So why worry when you can pray? Remember the text from Psalm 34: "I sought the Lord, and he heard me, and delivered me from all my fears." And so He will.

YOUR OUTLOOK DETERMINES YOUR FUTURE

Brethren, I count not myself to have apprehended:
but this one thing I do, forgetting those things which
are behind, and reaching forth unto those things
which are before, I press toward the mark for the
prize of the high calling of God in Christ Jesus.

–Philippians 3:13-14 KJV

Your outlook determines your future. This is a definite, provable fact. Your future is not determined by circumstances over which you have no control, but is conditioned by the attitude you have toward yourself, toward other people, toward the world, and toward God, to determine your future. It need not be merely the result of undisciplined circumstances.

Let me tell you about a friend of mine. He was standing one day on a street corner in a city, very disconsolate and indecisive. He had lost just about everything: his business, his home, and now he had lost even his car. He had just surrendered the keys to an official of the bankruptcy court. He was standing there hesitant, for he realized he must summon every dollar and was reluctant even to spend money for a taxi to take him to the home he no longer owned.

He was a man of some faith, although he had never exercised it to the fullest. But something prompted him to send up a little prayer for guidance. God acted, as He always does. A big truck came along, went past him a bit, then stopped. The driver leaned out and called, "Want a ride?"

My friend had never hitchhiked before, but he liked the looks of the truck driver, a big, burly, honest-looking fellow. So he climbed into the cab with him. He just had to talk to somebody, and the personality of this truck driver inspired confidence, so as they drove along he told him the whole story, down to the least detail. Then he added, "I have no future. All my future is in the past. The past is all I've got. There is nothing out ahead."

The truck driver said, "Sure, it's tough." Then he reached over with a big fist and poked my friend in the chest. "But listen, brother: You are tougher than it is, aren't you? And don't forget that God will help you." Then he added a very wise statement: "What happens to you in the future really depends on how you think of things from here on in."

In other words he was saying, "Your outlook determines your future." Parenthetically, my friend's case had a good outcome, for he took that truthful thought and built a new and a creative life with it.

Circumstances for any of us may at times become very difficult. Troubles may pile as high as the moon. They can either overwhelm you, or they can become an open door to a greater and more wonderful life. Everybody has essentially the same facts to deal with. One person takes those facts and makes something great of them. Another person takes the same facts—or rather they take him—and is destroyed in the process.

A gentleman who is very close to me, a relative in fact, and another young man of about the same age were caught in an intra-company political situation, and both were suddenly out of a job. They had counted on their jobs, for this company seemed to have every prospect of great advancement for them. But here they were, out, both of them.

What did the two men do? My relative sat down and said to the Lord, "I don't understand why this developed, but I know that You have an answer for me. So I'm going to have the attitude that there is something better in store for me; and the only way You could give it to me was to get me out of the situation I was in. Perhaps I was going to seed."

Then he took the directory of directors and other business reference books and made a list of one hundred of the top executives of great American business organizations. To these men he wrote a letter and enclosed his picture. (Some of us would do better not to put in a picture! But he is handsome enough for the picture to be an asset.) He told these presidents exactly what his record was. He showed me his letter, and I thought it was a masterpiece and absolutely honest. He summed up his case something like this:

"Maybe you could use a man like me. Here are my qualifications. As you will see, I have a few weaknesses." He had frankly enumerated them. "But I think the strong points outweigh the weaknesses. If you have a place for someone of my abilities, I hope you will let me hear from you while I am still available."

He had seven offers, one of which led him to the very thing in life that he could do best.

The other fellow had a nervous breakdown. He went all to pieces. And he hasn't made anything of his life even yet, I am sorry to say. But he could—it is never too late —if he would get the proper outlook.

When you face a mess of difficulties, it can be plenty tough—there is no denying it. But if you take the attitude and adopt the outlook that something great can be done with your trouble, you can do something great. If, on the other hand, you take the attitude that in this unhappy situation you have been discriminated against and everything is against you and it is all unfair, etcetera, then you just make yourself the victim of the adverse circumstances. Your outlook determines your future.

How, then, do you get the proper outlook? There are two things, I think, to do. First, let God guide you. Let Him put rightness into you. There is a lot of error in all of us. There is a great deal of error in you. Maybe there is even more in me. This problem is in everybody's life. Your possibilities of success and happiness depend in the long run on whether you have more of truth or more of error in you. Error in you will result in ineptitudes, mistakes, wrong talking, wrong thinking, and wrong doing. And when you are wrong, things naturally go wrong. This is part of why you should go to church, why you should read the Bible, why you should live with Christ. All these things help get more rightness into you. I don't mean moral rightness only, but perceptiveness, astuteness, understanding, penetration, insight, wisdom. The person who has rightness develops a good future. But if you are wrong, then things are bound to turn out wrong. Years ago, there was a fellow by the name of Louie who used to come to Marble Collegiate Church. Louie wouldn't mind my mentioning his name because he had a great experience. He got the notion that I was a skilled psychological counselor—which I never claim to be. But he kept coming around to see me. He was, by all odds, the most complex and mixed-up human being I had ever dealt with. He wasn't a bad man; he was just wrong, that was all. I would give him a suggestion and ask him to try. This he would do to the best of his ability and understanding, but he never got a satisfactory result. I tried everything I knew. It almost got so that when I saw Louie coming, I wanted to go the other way. He was a real problem, and I couldn't get anywhere with him.

One evening on my way to Allentown, Pennsylvania, to make a speech, I ran into Louie as I came out of the church. "I'd like to talk with you," he said.

"Well, I can't stop now, Louie. I have to go to Allentown right away."

"How're you going?" he asked.

"In this car."

"Well," he said, "that's great. I haven't anything else to do. I'll ride down there with you."

This certainly was the last thing that I wanted, but I sat back and listened as he talked, telling me the same old story, all the way to Allentown. Then, when I had made my speech and we started back, he began telling me the same story all over again.

About 11:00 PM, we came to one of those famous food emporiums that line the highways of America, and I suggested, "Louie, how about a hamburger?"

He said he'd like that. We went in and got two nice hamburgers all fancied up with relish and onions and everything. We were drinking coffee, and on our second hamburger, all of a sudden, to my embarrassment, Louie hit the counter with an enormous blow of his fist, making the silver rattle and the coffee swish out of the coffee cups as he exclaimed, "I've got it! I've got it! I've got it!"

"You've got what?" I demanded.

"I've got the answer to myself!"

"Well, brother," I said, "never in all my life did I know there was so much power in a hamburger!"

We went outside, and there in the moonlight, leaning against the car, Louie said, "At last I realize why everything goes wrong with me. It's because I am wrong *myself*. What else could you expect?"

I looked at him in amazement. It was one of the most dramatic flashes of insight I had ever seen a human being experience. And what did Louie do then? He knew he had to get the wrongness out of him. So, standing there by that automobile in the moonlight beside a great highway, he dedicated his life to Jesus Christ and asked Christ to come into him and change his thought processes. And Jesus Christ did. It wasn't easy to make the turn, but the turn was made. He had a new outlook, and as a result of the new outlook, he had a new future.

I don't want to oversimplify it. There are many factors and complexities in the human mind that determine the way we go and where we get. But one thing is sure: If you forget those things that are behind, as the Bible teaches, and reach forward toward those things that are ahead, pressing "toward the mark for the prize of the high calling of God in Christ Jesus," you have a future that is full of strength and hope and joy.

The second thing, second only to letting God put rightness into you, is to let God put strength into you too. Nobody who isn't strong—strong in his faith, strong in his spirit, strong in his morality, strong in his whole being—can ever hope to have a future.

I sometimes get concerned about the day and age in which we live, wondering whether we are still developing strong people like those who made this country great in days gone by. Are we developing a generation of permissive, weak people whose weakness could destroy the very fabric of the United States? Our national future is tied in with whether or not we have strong people. I thank the Lord that I shall never be a mother, because being a mother is the toughest job in the world, and I wouldn't be equal to it. What has a mother got to be? She has to be sweet, she has to be patient, she has to be gentle, she has to be understanding and long-suffering with her husband and with her children; she just has to be all these things. And at the same time there is another quality she ought to have: namely, strength. Many mothers do have it. But in this country today, we need more mothers with steel in them, because it is the duty of a mother to rear strong men and strong women.

A thought-provoking article appeared some months ago in the weekly newspaper *Our Sunday Visitor*. It is written by Mrs. Bobbie Pingaro and titled: "I Had the Meanest Mother in the World." Here are a few lines from it: "I had the meanest mother in the whole world. While other kids ate candy for breakfast, I had to have cereal, eggs, or toast. When others had Cokes and candy for lunch, I had to eat a sandwich . . . My mother insisted upon knowing where we were at all times. You'd think we were on a chain-gang. She had to know who our friends were and what we were doing. My mother actually had the nerve to make us work. We had to wash dishes, make beds, learn to cook, and all sorts of cruel things. My mother always insisted upon our telling the truth, the whole truth, and nothing but the truth, even if it killed us—and occasionally it nearly did. . . . None of us has even been arrested, divorced, or beaten his mate. Each of my brothers served his time in the service of this country. And whom do we have to blame for the terrible way we turned out? You're right, our mean mother. I am filled with pride when my children call me mean. . . . Because, you see, I thank God He gave me the meanest mother in the whole world."

Now the writer of that article had a real human being for a mother. She was a loving and rugged Christian mother who understood that it was her duty to raise her children strong, so as to give them power over their emotional, their mental, their physical, and their spiritual lives. And she knew that the only way to become strong people is by becoming disciplined people.

By too much permissiveness, you actually deny a young person his heritage. If you don't give him discipline, the world will discipline him and discipline him hard later on. Old and young alike, we all do too much complaining about the difficulties and hardships in human life. I don't like them any more than anybody else, but they are good for us. It is through suffering and struggle that we develop strength and become great human beings. And if you have this outlook, you can count on a good future.

Let me close with one more illustration. The scene is Centre Court at Wimbledon in London. A great crowd is gathered. An American girl has just won the women's singles tennis championship of the world. She is a tall, graceful woman. Standing there listening to the plaudits of the multitude, she sees walking toward her Elizabeth II, queen of England, holding the cherished cup of victory. She curtsies before the queen and receives from Her Majesty's hand this great sports honor. In this moment of triumph, her mind goes back to the early years of her life.

Born in New York of poor parents, she had had to struggle with one problem after another. While she was still a child, her family lived for a while on a little piece of land outside the city. At that time, she had an illness and was sickly and weak for a long time. One day her mother called to her and said, "Honey, see that stone down by the barn? I want you to move that stone up here so we can use it for a stepping-stone by the kitchen door."

"Mommy, I can hardly walk to the barn, let alone bring a stone up here," the girl said.

"Well," her mother told her, "you go down to the barn as best you can and start moving the stone. Even if you move it only half an inch in this direction, move it that much. Move it half an inch today and half an inch tomorrow, but start moving it."

The girl went down to the stone. She pushed it half an inch. She came back to the house exhausted. The next day she pushed it an inch and returned exhausted to the house. One fine day she pushed the stone five inches. It took her nearly two weeks to do what a child in normal health could have done in a few minutes, but finally came the day when, with flushed face, she got the stone to the kitchen door.

People muttered that her mother was a hard woman. Why didn't she carry the stone herself? Well, she may have been a hard woman, but she was a wise mother. She knew that things like moving that stone would make her daughter strong. By and by the girl did grow strong. The family moved back to Harlem. The girl became a tennis champion. Ultimately she became one of the greatest tennis players in the world. Her name was Althea Gibson. She had many difficulties, but she had the outlook of strength gained from her experience with a wise mother and from her faith in God.

Any future that lies out there for anybody is lined with difficulty. But whoever keeps his eye on Jesus Christ as the mark and reaches forward, having turned his back on the past, will move into a great and glorious future. Your outlook determines your future. So get a great outlook.

WHAT IS THERE TO MAKE LIFE GOOD?

For with you is the fountain of life;
in your light we see light.

—Psalm 36:9 NIV

Some time ago, after making a rather enthusiastic speech about this wonderful world and this glorious life, and how everything in general is good as I happen to see it, I was approached by an obviously off-beat representative of the younger generation, who said, "Don't make me laugh. What is there good about life anyway?" He never gave me a chance to answer, for he departed, and so did I. But his question lingered with me. What is there, indeed, that makes life good?

The answer, of course, is that there is plenty to make life good for those who are able to see it and able to take it. What this world is to you and to me and through us to other people depends, very largely, on our attitude toward it all, on our cast of mind, on the spirit with which we approach it.

The other night I was in Halifax, Nova Scotia, to give a speech to a large audience made up of salespeople and the general public. The people in charge suggested that I remain in my room at the hotel as long as possible and then come to the auditorium by taxicab. At about five minutes of eight—the meeting was to begin at eight—I got into a taxicab, little realizing that it was a twenty-minute drive. So the meeting was held up a bit.

Well, I gave the address of St. Patrick's Auditorium to the nice, clean-looking young fellow who was driving this taxicab. As we started, he asked, "There is a doctor from New York speaking there tonight, isn't there?"

"I guess there is," I said. "Why?"

"Well," he continued, "I would like to hear him, but I can't. I have to work tonight. I go to college during the day, Dalhousie University, and I drive this taxicab at night. My wife would like to go, too, but she is a nurse and she can't be off tonight."

"You are a hardworking young couple, aren't you?" I remarked.

"Yes," he said, "but don't be sorry for us. We are having a good time. We like it. But, you know, I would like to hear that man tonight."

"Well," I said, "you have the man right with you now. What is it you want to know?"

"Are you the man who is going to make the speech?"

"I am."

He turned around and looked at me. "It will take us fifteen minutes to get there. Can't you give me a rundown of the speech as we drive along?"

And I did. It took me forty-five minutes to give it in the auditorium and fifteen minutes to this man.

"I want to tell you something," he volunteered. "This is a wonderful world, and this is a wonderful time to be alive. Now," he continued, "you take my father. He always taught me to love God and to live the right kind of life and to have a positive attitude toward things. And my wife and I, we are going to do something with our lives. We just know we are."

I told him about my off-beat, far-out friend who could see nothing in life, who thought it was a "flop," a dismal failure, a "wash-out," and various other things.

The young man commented, "You know, I feel sorry for those guys. Somehow or other they are so mad at everybody and so mad at themselves that they've got all mixed up. I think we ought to try to convert some of them, don't you?"

It is refreshing to be visiting in a city, whether in the United States or in Canada or wherever else, and to find that there are people who have such a vital idea of life. That is why the Bible lives on from generation to generation. The Bible knows the score. The Bible writers knew everything about the rottenness and depravity in human existence. The Bible writers knew all about the evil in men. But the reason this Book does not become obsolete is that it also transmits the realization that God is good and the world is good, and there is a great deal of good in human beings.

In the thirty-sixth Psalm, verse nine (KJV), is the affirmation, "For with thee is the fountain of life." What a picture! A surging, sparkling fountain. *Thou (God) art the fountain of life.* And out of that fountain comes great goodness.

In life we have to balance one thing against another. We are aware, very painfully aware, that everything in this world today is not sweetness and light. And sometimes we have to deal with ugly facts. I have an editorial clipped from a prominent religious journal, and I cite this in order that you may balance the conditions it depicts against any superficial effervescence about life:

The writer says that many servicemen returning from foreign lands "see America from a wholly different perspective." In some cases "their long absence sharpens their awareness of America's moral decline" and "they gaze with bewilderment on a scene marked occasionally by riots, strikes, racial tensions, obscenity, sexual license, and spiritual atrophy." And: "The facade of affluence cannot conceal the desperateness of our plight and the speed with which we seem to be approaching the end of our nation's greatness." I am hearing this now more and more.

Well, now, I don't know whether I am willing to accept that appraisal, but it is a fact that the time is long overdue when people who believe in God and in Jesus Christ and in the Ten Commandments and in the moral standards of our civilization should rise up and do something about it. I am glad to say that we in Marble Collegiate Church are attacking current problems through spiritually oriented programs aimed at changing the lives of people as well as improving conditions.

But granting the deplorable trends mentioned above, it is also true, thanks be to God, that there are thousands upon thousands of members of the younger generation who instinctively in their hearts know that life is good and want what is good. The pity is that too often the churches fail to tell them that through the power and the grace of Jesus Christ, they can have life that is good and wonderful and ever new. In Switzerland last summer, while on vacation, I received a telephone call from a boy who told me he was an American soldier stationed in Germany. He asked if he could come to see me. Not knowing what it was about, I replied, "Well, I am only going to be here until tomorrow, and I haven't much time . . ."

"I assure you, sir, it is a life-or-death matter with me," he persisted. "Will you see me?"

"If it is a life-or-death matter, I surely will," I replied, "though I don't know how I can help you. How did you know I was here?" I asked. "Did you contact New York?"

"No," he said. "I have a couple of your books, and I know you go to Switzerland sometimes. I know you go to certain cities, so I have called around to those cities, praying that I might find you." He added that he was three hundred miles away and said, "I will be there in the morning."

"All right," I said, "nine o'clock."

At nine o'clock the next morning, a nice-looking American boy, about twenty-one or twenty-two years old, walked in. He seemed nervous. We secluded ourselves in a corner of the lobby and sat down. "What's the trouble?" I asked.

"I can't stand the kind of life I am living. It is hell! I can't live with it anymore. I've got to get away from it." And he described a not unusual kind of moral decline.

"Where are you from, son?" I asked him.

He said he was from Maine. "I've got to have help, Dr. Peale. I've got to have help. I fell for all the talk that this was the kind of life to live. But there is no fun in it. And I feel dirty. Dirty! What will I do?" And he asked nervously, "Can I get a cup of coffee here somewhere?" That is characteristic of many people when they are nervous. They've got to have either a cigarette or coffee. This fellow had to have coffee. So we went across the street to a little café on the corner.

This interview was taking place in Interlaken, Switzerland. There is a big meadow in the heart of the town, and towering over this meadow is one of the great mountains of the world, the Jungfrau ("Young Wife"). Like a coy young wife she often throws a veil over her face in the form of cloud formations. That morning, however, the veil had been cast aside and there she was, in all of her white, sparkling, radiant glory. We sat there at a table at the café. The boy gazed at the mountain and said, "I never saw anything like that." And he added, "That's the way I want to be: clean, like that!"

I had a glimpse of something of the depth of the boy's soul. He has it in him to be a tremendous leader of men, if he can be responsive to such cleanness and give expression to it. "You can be," I said, "if you will bring Jesus Christ into your life."

"Oh," he exclaimed, "thank God! That's what I wanted to hear you say!"

So apparently nobody else had said that to him. Why wouldn't they say that to him? He leaned over the table where we were having coffee and at my urging gave his heart to Jesus Christ. He told me he had one more day off. "Go up there among the mountains, where it is clean, and talk with God," I said. That boy now knows that not only is there real good in life but where to find it.

It is a great tragedy for the youth of the present generation that so many of them have never been pointed in this direction. What is the trouble with the older generation and with the Church that they have not been witnesses to the fact that this is truly the way of the good life?

Yes, what is there good in life? There is cleanness. There is peace of mind. There is serenity of heart. There is self-respect. All these are good things. And then, too, another thing that makes life good is that you never need be defeated in this world, never, even when you are old, or when you have had a lot of disappointments and frustrations and heartache or when things have gone against you. It is still good out there, life is. You can still recoup. You can still build again in this wondrous land of opportunity. I am constantly hearing criticism of the "establishment"—some bad, mean thing that holds everybody down. This country isn't perfect. Not at all. Who is perfect? But there is still great opportunity in this country, under God, under freedom, for a human being to say to himself, *With the help of God, who is the fountain of life, there is always something new and wonderful for me.* I was talking once with a friend, a man now who has since passed. He is Colonel Harland Sanders. He always wore a white suit and a black string tie. He had white hair and a white beard and carried a cane. His face was just written all over with kindness. He looks like, and is, in fact, a Kentucky colonel of the old school. All around this country you will see his picture, if you look for it, on many a restaurant where they serve Kentucky Fried Chicken—which is, according to him, "finger-lickin' good." And Colonel Sanders was one of the most generous of men. He was really a lovable man.

His father was a miner, back in the days when they didn't make much money mining. I think his father was killed in the mines and his mother had to go to work in a shirt factory. She had three young children, and Harland was given the job of being cook for the family—which later paid off with the fried chicken. He has worked very hard all his life. He had to leave school at the end of the sixth grade. He experienced the kind of poverty that has always existed in the Kentucky mountains and in Tennessee—at least in the poverty pockets. He grew up very, very poor. Finally he got a little restaurant going. Then they rerouted the highway, and he lost everything. That was when he was sixty-five years of age.

So he is sitting on his porch in Corbin, Kentucky, one morning, when the mailman comes up the walk and hands him an envelope from the United States Government. It contains his first Social Security check. Amount: $105. He is sixty-five, broke, and defeated. *My government is going to give me $105 a month so that I can eke out an existence,* he thinks. So he began to pray: *Dear God, You brought me into life for more than this. I ask You to guide me and also help me to help mankind.*

While he was praying, the thought of his special recipe for fried chicken came to him. He knew a particular formula. And he decided he would go out and see if he could sell franchises to this fried chicken. He had a car about ten years old, and he had a blanket. He toured the country, sleeping in the car when it was cold and wet, and sleeping out on the ground when it was dry. Sixty-five years old, undefeatable, a Christian who believed in the guidance of God and believed that not one of His children need ever be defeated.

In Salt Lake City, he sold his first franchise. For every chicken sold he was to get five cents. Later on there were six hundred franchised restaurants. At that point, when he was seventy-five, he sold most of his rights for two million dollars. The company that bought them then hired him at forty thousand dollars a year to be their goodwill ambassador.

Then, at eighty, this man walked among his fellows like a saint. It is not that he achieved a great financial success that makes his life story significant. It is that he knew life is full of good and that God is the fountain of life for everyone who will put his trust in Him. So when you think of the present-day world, how evil it may have become, how the old standards seem to have broken down, how mankind has reverted to the filth of Roman Empire days and wallows in it, remember also that there are beautiful mountains and rushing rivers and sounding seas and magnificent forests and that the stars come nightly to the sky and that the sun still goes down in the west in an effulgence of beauty. Remember also that there are good people, people reaching for the good, people who will not let anything overwhelm them, people who see the surging fountains of the waters of life and who wash themselves in them and become clean and fresh and restored. Be glad that you have life. It is a precious thing. It is awfully good. Keep it good as long as you have it.

THE POWER
OF HOPE AND
EXPECTATION

Why art thou cast down, O my soul? and why
art thou disquieted within me? hope thou
in God: for I shall yet praise him, who is the
health of my countenance, and my God.

–Psalm 42:11 KJV

There are two dynamic words that can change your life. Write these words in gigantic letters across the sky of your life, as you sometimes see skywriters writing advertisements against the heavens. Embed these two great words in your consciousness deeply. Condition your attitudes around these words until they become a motivational part of your whole being. Do this and your life will be good, very good, no matter how much pain or difficulty you may experience.

And what are these two magic words? What words can produce such dynamic results? I call it the power of *hope* and *expectation*. Set these words out clearly, these amazing words: *hope, expectation*.

The Bible, which is the wisest document ever known in human existence, which defies the ravages of time and change because it contains the truth that cannot be changed or invalidated, says in the forty-second Psalm, the eleventh verse: "Hope thou in God: for I shall yet praise him, who is the health of my countenance" (even healthy in the face) "and my God." What a text! There is power in it.

In the city of Detroit, there is a church on Woodward Avenue where a great minister by the name of Merton S. Rice preached for many years. I used to hear him when I was much younger. He was a great preacher and a giant of a man. Once he preached a sermon on this text, and a gifted sculptor was in the congregation. This artist was so impressed by what he heard that he conceived a bronze statue, which was later placed outside the church, depicting a man struggling against every difficulty, every obstacle, every pain, but was always looking up. And on the pedestal of the statue is carved: "I shall yet praise him." There is another text that is from the sixty-second Psalm: "My soul, wait thou only upon God; for my expectation is from him" (verse 5 KJV). That is to say, whatever you want from life, expect that God will give it to you and keep waiting on Him so that you will deserve to receive it. This is truth out of the wisest Book ever written.

So, there are the two words, *hope* and *expectation*. Do you know what can be done with words? It is amazing. Words spoken by an orator can electrify multitudes of people. Such was the power of the words of Demosthenes, William Pitt, Gladstone, Bryan. Words are alive. Words can destroy, and words can create. Words can break down, and words can build up. The kind of words you keep in your mind determines ultimately what you are, what you become. There is no power like that of words.

What are the words you use every day? Better get a piece of paper and write down the chief words you use. If you want a mirror of why you are what you are, look at those words. Words are far more than an assemblage of letters; words are symbols expressing life. Confucius, who was one of the wisest men who ever lived, was once asked what he would do if he could suddenly become the emperor of China and, as it used to be in the old days, have complete power of life and death over his subjects. What would he do? He said he would teach the people of China specific words that were creative. He knew that you can make or break yourself by words.

So here are our two words: *hope* and *expectation*. Mary Martin used to sing in *South Pacific*: "I'm stuck like a dope with a thing called hope, and I can't get it out of my heart." She personified expectation too. How is your hope? How is your expectation?

Expectation and hope can release the potential that is within us. The fact is—and you don't hear it said enough —that every one of us has more potential than we think we have. Everybody in the world ought to get up in the morning saying, "By the grace of God I've got some potential." You try that tomorrow morning and see what your wife does! She'll think you are a little balmy, but she will be glad, because that is why she married you: she saw the potential in you. It's there. Have you got to the point where you are willing to settle for yourself as you are? Don't answer "yes" to that!

A man the other day remarked with an air of great wisdom, "Well, you've got to take people as they are."

"I don't believe that at all," I said. "I don't believe in taking anybody as he is. Take him as he can be, as he ought to be."

CONFIDENCE

Don't you ever say to yourself, *This is it. This is what I am. I have to settle for what I am.* Settle for your potential. If you expect potential, if you hope for your greatest potential, you will bring it out. There isn't anybody who by application of these two great words, *hope* and *expectation*, can't live a bigger, more creative life.

Furthermore, individuals seem to react in direct ratio to the way they are treated. Psychologists have recently been studying this relationship and have called it the Theory of the Self-Fulfilling Prophecy. Some interesting experiments have been conducted by the Harvard University psychologist Dr. Robert Rosenthal, to prove the power of self-fulfilling prophecy. He took twelve students and gave each of them five rats, just plain old everyday rats, all of a kind. But the professor told six of the students that he was giving them the greatest rats in the whole history of rats. He told them that their rats all had great potential and that they could train these rats to do practically anything.

The other six students were told that their rats were the dumbest, most stupid rats that had ever been developed in the rat kingdom. The professor said he was sure the students couldn't do anything with such rats and he was sorry, he wanted to apologize—but he gave them their five rats just the same. The twelve students, over a period of six months, were to train their rats to go through mazes and do all sorts of contortions and maneuvers.

Well, at the end of the period the students with the rats presumed to be brilliant had developed the most marvelous rats imaginable. They could do anything. When food was placed at the end of the maze, they would go through every kind of maneuver and trick in order to reach the food. They performed brilliantly.

Of course, the rats knew nothing about this, but the students from the start had an idea that these rats were good.

On the other hand, the rats that the students training them regarded as dumb were lethargic, indolent, and lazy. They performed no tricks. They could hardly get their food.

The lesson is that even in a rat there is amazing power in expectancy. Expect the rats to come through—and they did. Expect them not to come through—and they didn't.

Maybe you find that experiment too bizarre to be convincing. Well, the same professor went into a poor area of San Francisco, where students were undisciplined, where they never produced, where they were problem children. He picked at random twenty-four children and divided them into two groups, as he had done with the rats. Now we are on a higher level; we are not on the rat level, but the human level. He put half of these children in the hands of certain teachers, telling them that these students had tremendous potential. He assigned the other twelve children to another group of teachers, telling these teachers that their children were lacking in potential, that they didn't have what it took and doubtless it would be impossible to accomplish anything with them. Then he prescribed a series of exercises for all these children to be put through.

He returned six months later to check on the results. The students in charge of teachers who had been told that they could expect great results from their students were doing spectacular work, whereas the other students were, if anything, even more desultory than before.

There are a lot of statements going around about how we can raise the quality of our citizenry today. I would just like to put forth the theory of self-developing, self-fulfilling prophecy. What people think you expect of them, they will deliver. And what your own psyche thinks you expect of it, it will deliver.

The development of a human being is illimitable if he hopes in God and expects from God. So there are two great words. Examine your words. What are the chief words that motivate you? Substitute *hope* and *expectation*.

We could talk on this theme for hours, for it has all kinds of possibilities. Hope. Expectation. With these two words you can overcome any defeat. No one really needs to be defeated by anything. I believe this! I wouldn't say it if I didn't. If you practice hope and expectancy, you can ride out whatever happens. My wife and I were in England for a little while last summer. And one typical English summer day—which means a cold, dark, dismal, rainy day: Have you ever read the weather forecasts in an English newspaper? They run about the same day after day: "Tomorrow: rain, fog, hail, wind, with a few bright intervals." Isn't that wonderful!— Well, on this day we didn't have many intervals, but it was a great day. We went down to Chartwell, Winston Churchill's old home, where he lived for many years and especially during the war. They have opened it now to visitors. A beautiful place it is, overlooking the wealds of Kent, with the greenest grass you ever saw, probably because it rains so much. You go through the house of a great man, left just as it was when he died.

I went through part of Churchill's library. I saw he had all kinds of books; so I looked to see if he had any of *my* books! I thought, *Wouldn't that be great.* But you know something? He didn't have, that I could find, a single one of my books! He did have one by another New York City minister, though, and I am going to congratulate him. Churchill seems to have read everything. He was a wide and prodigious reader.

Outside the house we were shown where Churchill used to stand every evening during the dark days of the Battle of Britain, big old hat on his head, chomping on the inevitable cigar, and watch the German bombers coming over in great waves. He could hear the reverberations of explosions in the center of London. From Chartwell he could see the flames. In a field nearby they still have one of the little Spitfires, the fighter planes with which the RAF fought off the Germans. Flying singly, one man in a Spitfire, they saved civilization—they and this indomitable old character. The woman who served as our guide was an old friend of the Churchills'. I asked her, "Did Winston Churchill ever lose hope?"

She laughed. "Churchill? No. Hope was built into him. He never expected anything but ultimate victory." That is why some men become immortal. They stand against every defeat, because they have hope and expectation built into them.

Well, you may think, *I'm not Churchill; I'm just a plain human being. I get assaulted by all the difficulties of life. Things that I plan go wrong. Things that I want don't come to pass. I am struck by trouble of one kind or another: illness, pain, weakness, prejudice, mistreatment.*

Certainly you are! But don't say you are going to let these things defeat you. Not when you have God, in whom you can hope, Who will help you yet to praise Him, and Who will put such a glow of victory and health in your countenance that it will be a thrill. *Every* day you can read about people who have practiced hope and expectation. In a magazine put out by American Airlines I read an article about Hayes Jones. I have not met Hayes

Jones, but I certainly hope I will sometime. He is the commissioner of recreation of the city of New York. He was working for American Airlines, but his accomplishments as a volunteer helper in physical fitness programs in Detroit attracted attention, and Mayor Lindsay borrowed him for two years to do this job in New York. The mayor is very smart to hire a man like this.

Back in 1960, Hayes Jones was the phenomenon of the year in high hurdles racing. He had won everything. He was the sensation of the hour. Naturally, he was picked for the Olympics, and he went to the Olympic Games at Rome with this worldwide reputation. But he failed to win a gold medal. In the 110-meter high hurdles, he finished third. It was a terrible disappointment, and the logic of the situation was that he should quit. There would be no more Olympics for four long years, and he had already won all the other coveted championships. That was the logic, but Hayes Jones said, "You can't be logical about something you've wanted all your life." So he started training again, three hours every day, seven days a week.

In the next couple of years, he made some new records in the sixty-yard and seventy-yard high hurdles. Then came the night of February 22, 1964, in Madison Square Garden. It was the sixty-yard high hurdles. He had announced that this would be his last indoor race. He ran it in seven seconds flat, tying his own previous record.

Then a strange thing happened. In those days, in the old Garden, runners, after crossing the finish line, disappeared under a ramp before they could slow down. When Jones walked back into view, he stood there with his head bowed. And seventeen thousand people stood in tumultuous applause. Jones wept. Many of the spectators wept too. Because a once-defeated man had made a comeback.

At the Olympic Games in Tokyo later that year, Hayes Jones ran before a crowd of one hundred thousand in the 110-meter high hurdles, one of the most grueling races in the whole field of sports, and he ran it in 13.6 seconds, finishing first.

Now he is teaching the youth of New York. Anything wrong with the youth of New York? There is nothing wrong with the youth except that a lot of people over a long period of time have been giving them the pernicious impression that they weren't intended by God to make something great of themselves. Americans love a man who was a loser but who will become a winner because of hope and expectation.

If you never stop fighting, you will never be defeated. So build up hope and expectation in your mind and in your heart. Use those great texts. You have heard them before, no doubt. If you haven't, take them now. Write them on your consciousness. "Hope thou in God: for I shall yet praise him," (yes, you will) "who is the health of my countenance, and my God" (Psalm 42:11 KJV). "My soul, wait thou only upon God; for my expectation is from him" (Psalm 62:5 KJV).

If you expect little things from God, you will get little things. If you expect nothing from God, you get nothing. But if you expect great things from God, He will draw out of you your self-revealing potential. You have it. You can release it. So take the words and walk with them and live with them and think with them and pray with them. Have the power of hope and expectation.

GO FORWARD WITH CONFIDENCE

For we are God's workmanship, created in
Christ Jesus to do good works, which God
prepared in advance for us to do.

–Ephesians 2:10 NIV

As we wind to a close, I'd like to mention that it is a fact that any human being who approaches the business of living with courage and confidence has two enormous factors going for him. And there are two special texts that apply. The first is this: "The Lord is the strength of my life . . . in this will I be confident" (KJV). Which is to say that you can depend on the Lord, come whatever, to give you strength. Those words are found in the twenty-seventh Psalm, the first and third verses.

The second text is from Isaiah, chapter 30, verse 15 (KJV): "In quietness and in confidence shall be your strength." This is a very subtle statement. No one is ever going to be confident if he is all stirred up on the inside. Agitation foments fear and self-doubt, but quietness, deep inner peace, produces confidence.

So how can one go forward with confidence? A part of the secret is to have a sound, humble awareness of the qualities within yourself that make for strength and for power. One of the tragedies of human existence is how little we realize the great power built into us by the Creator that is potentially available to us. So strongly do I believe this that I do not think anyone need ever be defeated by anything, no matter how difficult it may be. All he needs to do is to draw upon these enormous inner resources of strength that Almighty God has put within him against the hour of his difficulty.

Are you really acquainted with yourself? How long have you lived with yourself? Well, that is perhaps an embarrassing question. How long have I lived with myself? A long while. Do you and I know ourselves? Really? Your opinion of yourself can be entirely wrong. You may think of yourself as inadequate and weak, as having ability just to a certain level, and you may settle for that. But that is doing yourself a disservice, because within every human being there is greater capacity than anything he has ever dreamed of. You see evidence of this again and again.

I like to think that one of the purposes in going to church, taking with you your weaknesses, your feelings of inferiority, your sense of defeat, is to hear the power-packed words of the Scriptures that can shoot into you an enormous injection of spiritual adrenaline by which you are able to do things you ordinarily could not do and overcome difficulties that had seemed insuperable. "The Lord is the strength of my life . . . in this will I be confident."

William James, who without a doubt was one of the greatest persons who ever lived in this country and who is generally recognized, I believe, as the father of philosophical psychology, stated after long study of human beings: "Compared to what we ought to be—we are only half awake." Well, we're not supposed to be that way. It really is pathetic.

A scientist in a Midwestern university not long ago expressed the opinion that the average man uses only a fraction of his powers. The average man, he declared, would increase his efficiency by 50 percent. Now just think what would happen if we increased our efficiency by 50 percent. What wouldn't we do with life! Thomas A. Edison remarked that if we human beings would do all that we are capable of doing, we would literally astound ourselves. And why is it that we don't? It's because we have never been fully released. One of the great gifts of the Christian religion is to release human beings to the full potential of what God designed them to be. I have been preaching this for years, and I intend to go on preaching it as long as I can stand up, because I feel that today all too many churches neglect to tell the individual what, by the grace of God, he can be.

Many ministers seem to think that Christianity is merely a program for social action—social change—and that is all they preach. But Christianity is more than that. It does provide a blueprint for social change—don't ever think it doesn't. And we cannot go on having poverty among us or so much injustice or such living quarters as in the ghettos of our great cities. These conditions must change, and Christianity is dedicated to changing them. But it is also dedicated to helping the poor individual living in the midst of this world who feels defeated and discouraged and needs to be reminded of who he is and what he is. When he knows who he is and what he is, then he can live confidently.

A newspaper carried an item entitled, "There's a Fortune in Your Attic." According to this article, there are several billion dollars lying around in old trunks, mattresses, dresser drawers, and elsewhere in the form of unclaimed securities. Several billion! Once in a while you'll see an advertisement in the newspaper listing unclaimed bank accounts. Well, according to this story, an elderly woman, very shabbily dressed, came into the office of a big utility company and asked to see the treasurer. She carried a soiled manila envelope, and inside were some yellowed stock certificates—very old. She said to the treasurer, "I'm a very poor woman, I'm living from hand to mouth, and I need some money desperately. While rummaging around looking for something else I found these. I don't know where they came from; they must have been there a long time. They look like stock certificates. Do you think maybe you could lend me a little money on them?"

The treasurer took them and went back to the inner office. Later he came out beaming and told her that the certificates, forgotten for so long, were worth on the market as of that day sixty-six thousand dollars.

Now don't rush immediately to ransack old drawers and trunks and attics for securities, but if I may borrow the figure of speech "there is a fortune in your attic"—not in the attic of your house, but in the attic of that temple of the soul called the human mind. There is a fortune there in the form of potential strength and peace and power and joy and happiness.

"For we are God's workmanship, created in Christ Jesus to do good works, which God prepared in advance for us to do." God who created you told you that He gave you dominion—not over any person but over the circumstances of life. So don't go on, defeated and crawling through life on your hands and knees. We need a new emphasis on the greatness of man. We hear plenty about the wickedness of man, the littleness of man, the cruelty of man—and he has all these elements in him. But, as Wordsworth says, "Trailing clouds of glory do we come from God, who is our home." Essentially, man is a tremendous being—a marvelous creature. That means you. It means me. Greatness! In my study alongside of my desk I have a bronze bust of a gentleman by the name of William Shakespeare, who is known to all of you. As I sit there working on a sermon or a bit of writing, I frequently look into this bronze face of the Bard of Avon. Now I haven't the slightest idea what Shakespeare really looked like; I doubt that anybody has. But whoever made this bronze bust got something of the old boy's wisdom into it. There is a kind of quizzical look on the face, with a little half smile. The eyes, even though they are bronze, seem to be full of light, and it's as though he were asking, *Do you know what you're talking about? Do you believe in yourself?* He has talked to me a lot, Bill Shakespeare, and one thing he seems to tell me is to go out and tell people what they can be.

When I first came to Marble Collegiate Church, we had a basement downstairs that had been left unfinished since the place was built in 1854. It had only about a five-foot clearance; you had to duck your head to walk through. There were two or three brick crosswalks and I think five furnaces, all of which smoked at different times on Sunday morning.

Finally we excavated and replaced that antique basement with a beautiful hall. And in the course of the excavation, this bronze bust of Shakespeare was unearthed. Where it came from, nobody knows. One of my predecessors, Dr. Burrell, was president of the

Shakespeare Society of New York many years ago, and it may be that he received it as a gift.

At any rate, it was dusted off and the sexton put it in his office.

Walking by there, I used to see this bust of Shakespeare. One day I had with me a curator of the Metropolitan Museum of Art, a very learned man in his field. He stopped and asked, "What's this?"

"That's Shakespeare," I said.

He examined it, looked at the inscription on the back signed by the artist, and said, "Why, this is a very valuable piece of art. This was done by one of the greatest workers in bronze in this city about seventy-five or eighty years ago." Whereupon, with the consent of the sexton, I took it out of his office and put it in mine.

Now our denomination was established by the great reformer John Calvin, who was a tremendous teacher of man's greatness through the redemptive grace of Jesus Christ. And we have some rigid people in our denomination, ministers and others—not many, but a few. One of them came into my office one day shortly thereafter and inquired, "Who's that?"

"It's Shakespeare," I replied.

"Why do you have a statue of Shakespeare in the office of a minister?" he asked. "Why haven't you got John Calvin here?"

"If you want to know," I answered, "it's because we didn't find John Calvin in the cellar."

Well, what I am leading up to is that Shakespeare wrote: "What a piece of work is man! How noble in reason! How infinite in faculty! In form and moving how express and admirable! In action how like an angel!"

Which is to say, go forward with confidence, believe in your Creator, believe in the Lord Jesus Christ, believe in the sanctity and greatness of your own self and recognize the inherent power you have been given over everything—over weakness, over sickness, over old age, over opposition, over trouble. It's within you. Let the Lord Jesus bring it out. Don't hug it. That is tragedy—hugging it. Let it come out! An important element in going forward confidently is to live daringly. Faintheartedness always gets faint results. "Faint heart ne'er won fair lady." It never won any battles. Faintheartedness is destructive. Don't ever get to the point where you're excessively cautious. Of course a certain amount of sensible caution is required. Don't run out into the street without first looking both ways. But throw fear to the winds and live courageously.

Dare to be what you ought to be; dare to be what you dream to be; dare to be the finest you can be. The more you dare it, the surer you will be of gaining just what you dare. But if you go at things timorously, telling yourself, *I'm afraid I'll never make it* or *I just know I can't do it* or *I haven't got what it takes,* then you will get a result in kind. Dream great dreams; dare great dreams. Have great hopes; dare great hopes. Have great expectations, dare great expectations. "The Lord is the strength of my life . . . in this will I be confident."

A friend of mine sent us for Christmas last year an attractive new edition of a wonderful little book by William H. Danforth. Bill Danforth was chairman of the board of the Ralston Purina Company of St. Louis. I knew him well and admired him very much. In this book he tells about a great experience in his teens that changed his life. At that time he was a sallow, narrow-chested boy; he was weak; he was pathetically thin. He had been reared in swampy country where malaria was a rampant disease in those days. His folks worried about him and pampered him so much that he developed fears of chills and fever and got the notion he was fated to be a semi-invalid all his life.

Then one day at school a certain teacher who frequently gave the boys some strong talking-to on health singled out young Danforth and said to him, "I dare you to become the healthiest boy in this class." Now practically every other boy in the class was a real husky compared with Bill. But the man said to him, "I dare you to chase those chills and fevers out of your system. I dare you to fill your body with fresh air, pure water, wholesome food, and daily exercise until your cheeks are rosy, your chest full, and your limbs sturdy. I dare you to become the healthiest boy in the class."

Well, Bill Danforth took the dare—and he developed a splendid, robust physique. Seventy years after that time, in the lobby of the Jefferson Hotel of St. Louis where I had a little visit with him, I asked, "Mr. Danforth, just what did you do to get strong?" And so enthusiastic was he that despite his advanced age, he proceeded to show me all his exercises right there in the lobby of the hotel and insisted that I follow the exercises myself.

We soon had an audience of about twenty-five people around us. He said to them, "Everyone can be strong." And they believed it. And I believe it. He told me that he had outlived every member of his class. Dare to be strong!

Mr. Danforth in his little book tells about a salesman named Henry Woods. (This has to do with another kind of strength.) This salesman came to him one morning and said, "Mr. Danforth, I've had it. I never can be a salesman. I haven't got the nerve. I haven't got the ability. You shouldn't be paying me the money I receive. I feel guilty taking it. I'm quitting right now."

Mr. Danforth looked at him and said, "I refuse to accept your resignation. I dare you, Henry, to go out right now today and do the biggest sales job that you've ever done. I dare you."

He writes that he could see the light of battle suddenly blaze up in the man's eyes—the same surge of determination that he himself had felt when that teacher years before had dared him to become the strongest, healthiest boy. The salesman simply turned and walked out. That evening he came back and laid down on Mr. Danforth's desk a collection of orders showing that he had, in fact, made the best record of his life. And the experience changed him permanently. He surpassed his own record many times in the years that followed.

The important thing is that a brief, frank talk between two Christians bolstered up the confidence of the one who needed it. "The Lord is the strength of my life." He surely is! And "in this will I be confident." With this formula, go forward, always with confidence. Amen.

A NOTE FROM THE EDITORS

We hope you enjoy *Confidence* by Dr. Norman Vincent Peale, published by the Books and Inspirational Media Division of Guideposts, a nonprofit organization that touches millions of lives every day through products and services that inspire, encourage, help you grow in your faith, and celebrate God's love in every aspect of your daily life.

Thank you for making a difference with your purchase of this book, which helps fund our many outreach programs to military personnel, prisons, hospitals, nursing homes, and educational institutions. To learn more, visit GuidepostsFoundation.org.

We also maintain many useful and uplifting online resources. Visit Guideposts.org to read true stories of hope and inspiration, access OurPrayer network, sign up for free newsletters, download free e-books, join our Facebook community, and follow our stimulating blogs.

To learn about other Guideposts publications, including the best-selling devotional *Daily Guideposts*, go to ShopGuideposts.org, call (800) 932-2145, or write to Guideposts, PO Box 5815, Harlan, Iowa 51593.